RICK DEBRUHL AND

THE INSIDER'S GUIDE TO
MEDIA TRAINING

99 TIPS TO SURVIVE YOUR INTERVIEW IN THE DIGITAL AGE

Copyright © 2020
Rick DeBruhl and Kevin Riggs

All rights reserved. No part of this book may be reproduced in any form or by any electronic or mechanical means, including information storage and retrieval systems, without permission in writing from the publisher, except by reviewers, who may quote brief passages in a review.

ISBN # 9798692962614

1 2 3 4 5 6 7 8 9 10

Editing and Layout by: solfire@phoenix-farm.com

Cover Design: Nabin Karna nabinkarna02@gmail.com

** Editor's Note: because this a tip book, style decisions have be purposely made to make each tip a fast and informative read. This includes the choice to not use the Oxford comma, which has its place just not in a casual tip book. Please forgive us if we have crushed your heart by disrespecting the OC. We promise we will use it again for any academic and professional articles.

Printed and bound in the USA

DEDICATION

To our wives and families: Thanks for enduring all the long days, late nights and endless weekends while we worked in TV news.

And

To our fellow newsies: It was always an honor to be part of the tribe.

And

To Jim Hayes: The journalism professor and mentor who taught us to do the right thing and survive in a crazy business. In many ways, it all began with you. You may be gone, but you will always be fondly remembered.

PREFACE – MEDIA TIPS

When you prepped for an interview years ago, it was because a reporter from TV, radio or the newspaper (and occasional magazine) was going to be asking you questions.

Ah… the good old days. It's so much more complicated today.

The call could come from one of those "legacy" media outlets, or it could be from what we call "new media" which includes bloggers, a podcaster or social media influencers. Instead of sending a videographer to your home or office, they might just ask you to go online using Zoom or one of the other conferencing platforms which requires you to manage the technology.

There are also so many more types of reporters and interviewers. Many of which make no effort to hide their bias or agenda. The online world has a huge number of opportunities to spread your message, but it also requires that you be very aware of the interviewer and platform.

Things move fast now. Reporters are often expected to file their first report **_before_** they get to a major news event. They no longer wait for the 6pm newscast or the morning's print edition of the newspaper. Everything must be filed right now.

Doing any interview with the media is a little bit like parachuting out of an airplane. Once you step out the door, you can't go back. That doesn't mean something bad is going to happen. After all, plenty of people skydive every day and have a wonderful experience. That's because they do the right planning before the jump to make sure they're ready.

Whatever the media platform, you need to do the same thing for your interview. A little careful planning can make for a safe landing.

This book is designed to help you safely pack your chute and get you through what might be your first media experience.

Together we have more than eight decades of TV experience. We've interviewed literally thousands of people. We've also been on the other side getting interviewed. We've coached people through their first interviews, and we've worked with experienced professionals who just wanted to hone their skills.

Whether it's your first interview or your 100th, this book is designed to help you not just survive your media experience but hopefully thrive as well. Each page has simple advice that you can digest quickly to help ace your interview.

Read through the book today and then keep it handy for when the reporter comes calling. Don't try to memorize everything before the interview starts, just read a few tips to refresh your memory.

This book's goal is simple. We want you to be both ready… and relaxed.

Pretty much the same advice you'd get from a parachute instructor.

How to use this Book

You're busy. You barely have enough time to squeeze the media interview into your schedule.

That's why this book is perfect for you.

The reality is that we could have written a lot more about how to prep for interviews. However, we wanted something that would be quick and easy to digest. It won't take long to read this entire book. It **will** give you plenty of foundation to remember for any media interviews that come along.

Most important, if an interview request comes out of nowhere, and suddenly you can't remember all 99 tips, just take a moment to open a few pages and get some quick advice. Read the ***Too Long; Didn't Read*** page at the front of this book to refresh your memory in less than a minute.

There's also a great workbook section at the back of the book. It's a great way to plan for your interview. It lets you write down your headline and your sound bites so that you can sound so very eloquent when the reporter arrives.

Needless to say, we can't begin to cover every possible scenario. Each reporter, each interview and each topic is different. Think of these as general guidelines that will get you through the vast majority of interview situations.

We've also included a section to help you understand the person who is doing the interview. Having some knowledge about what their lives are like will help you when you're on the media hot seat. As you read through this, you'll also detect that we have respect for reporters. Together we have more than six decades of experience in the news trenches. We've worked alongside, and competed against, the full range of journalists. We can tell you that most of them are honest and forthright. They want to fairly cover every story they're given. Their lives are driven more by deadlines than agendas. There are absolutely a few bad apples in the bunch, however you can assume that the reporter who shows up at your door is a responsible individual and your interview will likely begin, and end, in a positive way.

Too Long; Didn't Read

In a hurry? Here are quick tips for your media interview:

- Dress the way you would for a job interview. Subtle and understated is best. Avoid loud colors and big patterns.

- What would your headline be? Before the interview starts imagine what the headline of the story will say. That will help to refine your message.

- Answer questions honestly. That doesn't mean you have to say everything, but you have to assume that the truth will eventually emerge.

- Remember to pause. When you get asked a question, don't just blurt out an answer.

- Know the show and the interviewer. Do a little research before you say yes. Make sure you understand who is asking the questions and the type of program this is for.

- No jargon! Avoid using terms that people outside of your industry might not understand.

- Everything is on the record.

- Look at the interviewer, not the camera.

- Make sure you know if the interview is live or recorded.

- Don't say "No comment" or walk out of the interview.

- Use analogies to explain complex issues.

- Shorter answers are better. Yes or No isn't enough, but don't drone on.

- Beware of the impulse to speculate. If you don't know, say so.

- Practice your main points beforehand to ensure you're speaking in a manner authentic to you.

Table of Contents

Dedication 3
Preface – Media Tips 4
   How to use this Book 6
   Too Long; Didn't Read 7

THE PREP 11
   #1 Why Make Time for this Interview? 12
   #2 Access Equals Goodwill 13
   #3 What Would Your Headline Be? 14
   #4 The Sound Bite 15
   #5 Making a Great Sound Bite 16
   #6 Questions in Advance? 17
   #7 Can I Send a List of Questions? 18
   #8 Be Early 19
   #9 Mock Interviews Are Important 20
   #10 Don't Expect to be Perfect 21

THE LOOK 23
   #11 What Not to Wear 24
   #12 What to Wear 25
   #13 Use a Mirror 26
   #14 Powder Up! 27
   #15 Slow Down 28
   #16 Pauses are Important 29
   #17 Stay Calm 30
   #18 Don't be Confrontational 31
   #19 Don't Walk Out 32
   #20 Good Props, Bad Props 33

THE PROCESS 35
   #21 Understand the Media 36
   #22 Legacy Media Matters 37
   #23 Beware of Off the Record 38
   #24 Breathe! 39
   #25 Brain Freeze 40
   #26 Expect to be Interrupted 41
   #27 Live vs. Recorded 42
   #28 Look at the Interviewer 43
   #29 Where to Look in the Studio 44
   #30 Understand the Deadline 45
   #31 You're Always on Camera 46
   #32 Survive a News Conference 47

#33	Stay in the Moment	48
#34	Know Your Media Protocol	49
#35	Phone Interviews	50
#36	Editorial Boards	51
#37	Controlling an Interview's Tempo	52
#38	Breaking News Broke Your Story	53

THE PLATFORM 55

#39	The Interview Starts at Hello	56
#40	How Much Detail to Offer?	57
#41	Paint a Picture	58
#42	Email Interviews	59
#43	Use a Landline	60
#44	Smiling for Radio and Podcasts	61
#45	Know the Show	62
#46	Zoom Interviews	63
#47	Podcast Interviews	64
#48	Short Morning Show Interview	65
#49	A 30 Minute Talk Show	66
#50	A 60 Minute Interview	67
#51	Are Trade Interviews Different?	68

THE MESSAGE 69

#52	Your Goal	70
#53	Focus on Your Message	71
#54	How to Pivot	72
#55	Why 'No Comment' is a Loser	73
#56	Offer Solutions	74
#57	Color, Not Play-by-Play	75
#58	How to Apologize	76
#59	You are the Expert	77
#60	Use Analogies	78
#61	Beware of Speculation	79
#62	Numbers are Great	80
#63	Take a Position	81
#64	Is it a Crisis?	82
#65	Close with a Key Message	83

THE INTERVIEW 85

#66	An interview Is not a Conversation	86
#67	Answer in Complete Sentences	87
#68	Answer the Question	88
#69	Be Honest	89
#70	An interview isn't a Deposition	90
#71	Keep it Short and Sweet	91
#72	Answer Even When You Can't	92

#73 Loaded Questions 93
#74 Crisis Interviews 94
#75 Can I start Over? 95
#76 Don't Repeat a Negative 96
#77 No Jargon! 97
#78 Answer the Tough Question 98
#79 Candidate Interviews Are Different 99
#80 It's Okay Not to Know 100
#81 Nail the Dismount 101

THE REPORTER 103

#82 Reporters: Enemy or Friend 104
#83 Understand the Reporter 105
#84 Journalists' Code of Ethics 106
#85 Deadlines Not Agendas 107
#86 Beware the Blogger 108
#87 Know the Interviewer 109
#88 Reporters Repeating Questions 110
#89 Hostile Questions 111
#90 Ambush Interviews 112
#91 Machine Gun Questions 113
#92 Don't Fill the Silence 114
#93 The Photographer is Your Friend 115

THE AFTERMATH 117

#94 Digital Corrections 118
#95 No Going Back! 119
#96 When Will It Air? 120
#97 Follow Up 121
#98 Watch the Interview 122
#99 They Only Used 15 Seconds! 123

BONUS TIP - Robot Journalism is Coming

Media Interview Work Sheet 125
About the Authors 127

THE PREP

#1
Why Make Time for this Interview?

We're all busy. It seems as though reporters are always in a rush. When they call, they're always battling a deadline and need to talk to someone right away.

What about you? You've got deadlines of your own to meet as well. It might be easy to feel some resentment and to wonder if you really need to set aside your projects and assignments in order to deal with a sudden media request.

The thing to remember is that while that media request may seem aggravating or inconvenient, it represents an important opportunity to communicate with your audience, whether it be customers, lawmakers, regulators, business colleagues or the public at large. While it is easier these days to tell your story through social media channels (such as Facebook, Twitter or Instagram) traditional, earned media coverage remains extremely important as a credible source of information.

What you always need to ask yourself is whether it's more important to complete a pending project or hold a scheduled meeting, and whether that's worth passing up a media opportunity that might carry great dividends for delivering your message or your point of view.

Of course, if it's a critical or negative story that will affect your credibility or your organization's reputation, it's even more important to respond. Reporters will tell their story with or without your input.

When a journalist calls, the clock is ticking, and the story won't wait.

Bottom line:

Don't squander an important communication opportunity.

#2
ACCESS EQUALS GOODWILL

If reporters appear to be always racing against the clock, it's because they are. Impatience is inevitable. And that has never been truer than in the current media landscape. Journalists now have to gather and prepare multiple stories—text, video, photos—for broadcast, print and digital platforms. The deadlines are relentless.

Against that backdrop, it's no wonder that journalists are grateful to those who accommodate their time constraints. The simple fact is that access equals goodwill. If you make yourself available consistently upon request, it doesn't guarantee what the story will look like, but it does improve your odds of being satisfied with the outcome.

When I was a political reporter, the leader of the Senate was very responsive to media requests. Yes, he liked the spotlight, like many politicians. But it wasn't just ego. He also recognized the value of leveraging that coverage to boost his policy priorities.

By contrast, the leader of the Assembly was aloof and disagreeable. He wasn't just resistant to media coverage but was openly hostile to it. He wouldn't make time.

The coverage by the capitol press corps often reflected that dynamic. Stories needed to be written, so the people willing to speak were interviewed more often. Reporters are human beings, and the topics they covered, the stories they wrote, tended to focus on the Senate.

Was it favoritism?

I don't believe so. You can't underestimate the value of goodwill, generated by willingness to grant access.

#3
What Would Your Headline Be?

Writing headlines is a tough job. Someone has to condense an entire story into just a few words that are both accurate and compelling.

While a newspaper or website usually writes the headline after the fact, you should think about it before the interview. Ask yourself: WWYHB - **What would your headline be?**

It's another way of considering ahead of time how to define the core of the story that you want to tell. If your ideal headline is, *Proposed Tax Bill is a Job Killer*, that gives you the ability to draft a road map that leads to or underscores that conclusion. It gives you the means to develop a series of points that, put together with supporting facts, build a specific case and leave the impression that you want.

It's a bit like reverse engineering. You've got a final product or story in mind. You just have to develop the process to get there! Envisioning the headline helps to define that process and to crystallize the story you want. It's a way to encourage message discipline.

Don't draw the wrong conclusion here.

The reporter isn't going to ask what the headline should be. And you can't expect that a news story will turn out exactly the way you want. One of the biggest complaints from readers is about the real-world headline and whether it accurately summarizes the story. Just make sure that the headline you design is something that can be accurately supported with facts and information.

#4
THE SOUND BITE

The sound bite gets a bad rap these days. You can almost hear people sneer as they say that phrase. The reality is that we often digest information and remember things in sound bites. It's just the way our brain is wired.

In simple terms, a sound bite is a short impactful statement. In the TV and radio world they usually last between 5-15 seconds. In the newspaper world they're simply referred to as quotes, but they have the same structure and function. A good reporter will instinctively listen for statements they know will work well as a sound bite or quote. It's almost as if a bell goes off in their head when they hear one. Newspaper reporters will invariably type faster when a great quote comes out of your mouth.

Trying to fight against sound bites is useless. Unless they're shooting a documentary, news broadcasters will always break up your interview into short snippets. That means your job is to give them a great sound bite that accomplishes your goal. It's a statement that's made for TV because you designed it that way. Practice them and rehearse how you'll say the words.

It's important to remember that sound bites can be your friend, or they can be your enemy. Used properly they get your message in front of large numbers of people watching or reading.

On the other hand, say the wrong thing and it could potentially drag you or your company down.

#5
MAKING A GREAT SOUND BITE

Here are some specific tips for making a great sound bite:

1. The best sound bites are between 5-15 seconds long.

2. A sound bite only has one thought or concept. Don't try to cram everything in.

3. Sound bites use simple language that everyone can understand. No jargon or acronyms.

4. Start with your strongest statement. Don't bury your sound bites in the middle of a long answer.

5. Let your body language back up the sound bite. If it's intense, lean forward. If it's whimsical, include a smile. If you're making a point, use your hands.

6. Sound bites are complete sentences.

7. Practice what you're going to say. The more you know your key points, the less likely you are to ramble and lose the sound bite.

8. Don't use sound bites to avoid something. They can be used against you!

9. Strong words. Use words like *must, will, absolutely, incredible or huge*. The sound shouldn't just be *noisy*, it should be *deafening*.

10. Absolutes. Sound bites make it clear you believe something is going to happen. People will die. Mankind will endure. Peace will come. Just say it in a full sentence.

11. Analogies are effective. There's a reason we all remember "Life is like a box of chocolates…"

12. Make it visual. Is the issue affecting 60,000 people? That's how many people were at the 2020 Super Bowl. Why is 25 people important? That's how many are on a major league baseball team.

#6
QUESTIONS IN ADVANCE?

One question reporters are repeatedly asked is if they can supply a list of questions before the interview. It seems like a reasonable request. After all, it will help you prepare for the interview. Let's make one thing clear right away: with a few rare exceptions, you're not going to get questions in advance.

If asked, reporters are willing to provide some background on the story they're working on, what role you'll play in it and the general areas of discussion they want to cover. What they won't be willing to do is send a list of prepared questions.

A large part of the reason for that is because they don't actually have a list. The most experienced journalists will have some basic questions in their head for the story they're pursuing but much will also depend on asking follow-up questions. They're listening to the answers provided to determine what direction the interview may go.

Reporters also don't want to have an interview request be determined based on whether you like all the questions.

There are exceptions to this practice. Trade publications, for example, are often receptive to submitting questions in advance. And for the sake of efficiency, more news outlets are now willing to provide questions for an interview that's conducted entirely by e-mail.

But for the majority of interviews, getting a sneak peek at the questions isn't in the cards. If you're confident about the subject, that shouldn't matter.

#7
CAN I SEND A LIST OF QUESTIONS?

It is perfectly fine to send a reporter a list of questions before your interview. Just don't expect they'll use them.

Back in my reporting days I received lists of questions all the time before an interview started. To be honest, I sometimes found them extremely helpful. Occasionally the list raised an issue that I hadn't thought of. In reality, I rarely used them verbatim. Part of it was simply hubris of not wanting to be told what to ask, and part was simply because I'd already assembled a list of questions in my head. Don't feel slighted, even when the newscast producer handed me a list of questions, I still went off on my own.

The one common exception to this rule is during morning show live interviews. Sometimes I wouldn't meet the person I was interviewing until just moments before we went live. Fortunately, we would often get a list of questions sent to us by PR people and we'd use that as the foundation for our interview.

Podcasters also like getting sample questions. While some podcasters are great at keeping the conversation flowing, others need a list of standby questions to keep handy.

So yes, prepare your list of questions. It can't hurt, and it might even help. Make sure they might have some news value that would give the audience new information. Just don't expect the reporter to use them.

#8
BE EARLY

Reporters never have enough time. The clock starts ticking even before they start their workday. They may be doing a story about a topic that they know absolutely nothing about and need to learn some basics on the run. And that running may include endless phone calls to find just the right person for an interview. I ate plenty of lunches at my desk because I just didn't have time to go someplace.

If you're their next interview, showing up late could launch a series of dominos that impact that reporter's day. Trust me, I've sat there and watched the clock while waiting for someone. I was doing mental calculations about how much time was left for me to finish the story to meet my deadline.

Why not make everyone's day a little better and show up just a little bit early? It's not just the reporter who benefits.

Being early will help you as well. You won't arrive at the interview all flustered or out of breath. You'll have a few calm moments to think about what you're going to say. You may even get a chance to spend a few extra minutes talking with the reporter. It will help build a rapport and may give you time to suggest something for that story or in the future.

Being early is even more important for a live TV interview. Not only will the producer panic today, but they'll think twice about asking you to come back.

#9
MOCK INTERVIEWS ARE IMPORTANT

You've reviewed your key messages, tried to anticipate questions, and framed the issue in your mind. It's all great preparation for the upcoming broadcast interview that'll be conducted live. What other step is missing? Practice. You know the adage: Practice makes perfect.

It's always smart to work through your remarks verbally. It's great practice, and you can do it any number of ways. Talk to the mirror, enlist the help of a family member to listen, or use your phone's camera to record and play back your anticipated delivery.

Even those who have years of experience with speaking on television find this practice useful. It accomplishes several things.

By speaking your answers out loud, it gives you the always important opportunity to edit yourself. You'll hear ways to abbreviate and summarize points that didn't occur to you before. In a pre-recorded interview, that wouldn't matter so much; the reporter would take on the editing. For live remarks, putting yourself on a "word diet" greatly enhances your value.

Another benefit of practice is that it allows you to customize your remarks to match your real voice; to more closely match your actual conversational style. You want to be authentic. What's written down often doesn't work when expressed verbally.

Practicing also allows you to avoid the mistake of trying to memorize everything.

What you're doing is familiarizing yourself with key points and ways to express them in a genuine way.

#10
DON'T EXPECT TO BE PERFECT

Professional speakers often talk about how there are three different speeches:
1. The speech you plan to give
2. The speech you actually give
3. The speech you wish you'd given

I can tell you right now that you'll probably feel the same way after you do your media interview.

You'll plan and practice your talking points. You'll rehearse with a co-worker or your spouse (or with the video app on your phone). You'll go over the notes just before the interview so you have all the important details.

Whether it's print or broadcast, the actual interview will likely drift out of your control. It might be because the interviewer had questions you didn't anticipate. Or it might be that you just couldn't remember all the facts you'd crammed into your head the night before.

When it's over and the reporter has gone, you'll wish you could do it all over. You realize that you left out some important fact or that you could have phrased something differently.

So, before it ever happens, I want you to promise not to beat yourself up. No one is perfect. The mere fact that you're reading this book shows that you're doing your homework. You're making an effort to do a great job.

Don't get me wrong, if you make a factual mistake that needs to be corrected, fix it. But go into the interview knowing that you'll do the best you can. It will help calm you down and that *will* make a difference.

THE LOOK

#11
WHAT NOT TO WEAR

Fashion is very subjective. The dress one person loves, someone else hates. While I would never attempt to give fashion advice, I *am* very qualified to tell you what you shouldn't wear during your TV interview.

Your goal during that interview is, first and foremost, to make sure people are listening to your message.

Colleagues have told me the story of a news conference where an engineer was being recognized for a prestigious space-related award. As a lab worker, he wasn't expected to show up in a coat and tie.

The problem was, he appeared on camera while wearing a colorful t-shirt that featured images of women who were ... well ... dressed for a visit to the beach. In this case, what he was wearing attracted so much attention, and criticism, that it drowned out the news about the award.

That's an extreme example, yet it illustrates a basic point: you never want to distract from your story by having people talk about what you're wearing.

So, let's start with the basics. Avoid bright colors. That neon purple dress may stand out at a party, but it will come off as radioactive on TV. Try not to wear white or black. The camera isn't as good as your eye and can't make out details in those colors.

You'll want to avoid big geometric patterns and small intricate designs as well. Big patterns are just brash and the small designs (like herringbone) create an unusual effect. Big stripes aren't a great look either.

It's usually better to overdress, than underdress.

#12
WHAT TO WEAR

If your interview will be photographed in any way, you need to take a moment and think carefully about your look.

Whether it's for TV, video podcast or just still photography, subtle is the key. Muted colors work best. At the same time, make sure it's something that you feel good wearing. You want to appear confident during the interview and that starts with your look. The best rule of thumb is to think about what you'd wear to a job interview. Professional and understated is always a good style.

A lot of outfits look great when you're standing yet rumpled when you sit. Make sure you test it both ways.

It may seem silly to mention shoes that are rarely seen, but make sure they're comfortable. You want to be focusing on the questions not the pain in your toes.

Consider bringing an extra outfit. I recently hosted an online video event and brought two coat-and-tie combos so the producer could choose.

Having said that, if your personality is tied to a particular look, then go for it. After all, it's important that you are authentic. If Hawaiian shirts are your signature style, then that's what you wear. Just understand that some folks will be thinking more about the palm trees in the pattern than what you're saying.

One more thing, no matter how bright the sun may be, ditch the sunglasses during an interview. The audience wants to see your eyes, not some dark or mirrored lenses.

Bottom Line:

Eliminate distractions so your words prevail.

#13

USE A MIRROR

When I first started in TV news, I worked at a very small television station. At 11pm, I did news, weather, and sports which I also wrote. In fact, I was the only news person in the building during the evening hours, which made things rather hectic. One night I rushed onto the set and started the newscast by reading a brief intro before tossing to our first story. I was immensely proud I had managed to get everything done. There was just one problem. I had buttoned my shirt but didn't pull up my tie. It was hanging about four inches below my neck. I looked like a complete buffoon. None of the other crew noticed because they were busy with their own jobs. In fact, it was my wife who called from home and told them.

All it would have taken was one quick look in the mirror and I would have avoided a major embarrassment.

You'll get plenty of advice about what you should wear for your TV appearance. The most important thing you need to remember is that you must look in a mirror before you begin. The TV reporter might not tell you t you have broccoli in your teeth or that your collar is flipped the wrong way.

It matters for two reasons:

First, you don't want to feel foolish when you watch your interview on TV.

Second, you want the audience focusing on your message. Not the broccoli.

#14
POWDER UP!

During my time in TV news I used to joke that I was one of the few guys who could come home with makeup on my collar and my wife was actually happy. It's not an accident that news anchors usually look good. They make it a point to wear the right clothes and to use makeup.

I'm not saying you need to get carried away in the makeup department, but you should absolutely use a little powder on your face during your interview. The oils on your face create shiny spots on your forehead and nose. It's amazing how much better you look when the shine is gone.

Obviously, this isn't news to most women. There's a multi-billion dollar industry directed at helping ladies improve their complexion. Guys, on the other hand, routinely dismiss the need for powder. They don't use it in the real world, why start now? It's because TV isn't the real world. It magnifies flaws. Just take a moment to read about how Richard Nixon's lack of makeup impacted his 1960 debate with John F. Kennedy. You don't want to be the shiny one.

Here's a word of warning about makeup: Don't use too much. Modern high definition cameras are great at showing every detail. Put on too much makeup and every bit will show.

Once again, you want to avoid distractions. If people are focusing on why you're using so much makeup, they're not listening to what you have to say.

#15

SLOW DOWN

When it comes to talking, I'm a speed demon.

I'm just one of those people who has a habit of cramming too many words into 60 seconds. It's something I've had to work to improve during my entire TV career, and I'm still not done. Before I'm about to do a live event, my wife regularly gives me the same advice: *slow down!*

I want you to remember her advice before you do an interview with the media. That doesn't mean you should slow your speech down to a pedantic crawl. You just want to make sure that you're not racing along so fast that people can't keep up with what you have to say. You should record yourself answering questions and see if it sounds fast to others.

Not only are you more understandable, it allows your brain a little extra time to formulate what you're going to say. Your mind is always moving faster than your mouth. That's a good thing because it allows you to formulate your next sentence. There's no reason for the mouth to try to catch up.

And there's another important reason.

Research shows that people believe fast talkers are actually **less** intelligent. They believe motor mouths are showing insecurity and low self-esteem. Not exactly the image you want to project during your TV appearance.

You definitely want to make sure you have energy. It will show you have passion for the topic. Just don't convert that energy to speed talking.

#16
PAUSES ARE IMPORTANT

It's amazing how much impact a little pause can have. A speaker's voice is rolling along when suddenly they stop. That moment of silence causes your brain to react. Your attention is refocused as you try to understand why. That's when a great speaker delivers a statement that has a huge impact. It's like the moment after a baseball is hit towards the outfield, and everyone wonders what will happen next.

Pausing during your interview has the same effect. You build to a certain moment, and then stop. It shouldn't be a long pause, just enough to force the listener to refocus.

Of course, the problem is that you're probably a little nervous. There's plenty of research about why people speed up their speech. Sometimes it's because they just want to get it over. Other times it's our brain over-processing and thinking that we're talking too slow. And then there are those people who just always talk fast.

Use the pause. Not only can it have great dramatic effect, but it can also be calming. It gives your brain a moment to think about what's coming next.

Finally, if it's for broadcast, there's a technical reason to pause during your interview. When the editor is trying to put the pieces into story form, they need pauses between sentences. A good editor can chop you off in mid-syllable, but you want to sound like someone who completed their thought.

So, remember.

Pause!

#17

STAY CALM

I recently heard a news conference where a TV reporter kept asking the same question over and over. His goal was to get a sound bite that either answered the question (in a way the reporter wanted) or showed the interviewee was getting frustrated (and must therefore be incompetent or hiding something).

Frankly, this situation won't happen to a lot of people. Most interviews are pretty calm and boring. The reporter asks questions and you answer. But when the topic is controversial, the rules change. Reporters will often ask the same question again and again.

Should you ever end up in that situation I'm going to suggest that you do the hardest thing you can imagine: I want you to stay calm. The moment your frustration boils over, you run the risk of saying something that could damage your reputation or the company you represent. And trust me, that's the sound bite that will be used in the story. It isn't easy. You're on the very public hot seat; it feels embarrassing. Just find that Zen-like happy place and stay calm.

Your answer may be very short. You can say that you don't have all the information just yet or that your organization has done the best it could under the circumstances.

You can still show concern for those affected, but being both concise and calm will make you sound very rational.

If that portion of the interview ends up on TV, people will wonder why you were being badgered.

#18

Don't be Confrontational

There's an old quote that says you should never get into an argument with someone who buys ink by the barrel. It basically means you want to avoid fighting with a newspaper that has lots of column inches to fill or a TV station that needs to fill hours of time every day. Your interview is not the time to let your frustration with the news media or the reporter asking questions to whip you into a frenzy.

I've seen it happen over and over again. The person being interviewed is frustrated about something and snaps back. They think that their insightful logic will shine through. It rarely works that way. After all, it's the reporter who gets to write the story. Even if they did make a mistake, they're not likely going to use something that makes *them* look bad. They're going to let you look like the loose cannon.

One of my personal peeves was when someone would tell me that something "wasn't a story" or that it's "fake news." The fact that a reporter is talking with you means it's now a story. No amount of arguing will change that. Worse yet, if it's a broadcast interview, you're going to come off as the angry person.

Getting confrontational with a blogger could mean a string of posts that continue the pain.

Your goal is always to make sure your message is heard. The interview is a great opportunity to achieve that goal. Don't blow it by getting confrontational.

#19

Don't Walk Out

The fastest way to become the lead story in a newscast is to rip off your microphone and storm off during a TV interview. It doesn't really matter how important the story was that day. You just made it bigger and better by adding theatrics.

Sometimes it really is your fault. You're getting peppered with the same question over and over because you're not actually giving an answer. On the other hand, I've heard plenty of TV reporters who I thought were truly belligerent in the way they kept pounding away at a particular issue.

Whatever the case, you don't want to allow your frustration to bubble over into something explosive. The moment you proclaim, "This interview is over!" and walk off, you've sealed your fate. You may have thought you were taking control of the situation, but in reality, you simply showed that you're easily flustered.

You have to remember that you agreed to do the interview. Once the camera is on, everything you say is fair game, even if the reporter changes the rules in mid-stream. This is true for zoom interviews and video podcasts as well.

Think of it as if you're dealing with a cantankerous child. You need to be the adult and maintain your composure.

Don't get me wrong, that's not easy when you're in a confrontational interview. Sometimes just taking a deep breath and at least looking calm on the outside will prevent your anger from making you a lead story.

#20
GOOD PROPS, BAD PROPS

During my TV reporting career, I loved to use props. It was something that I would hold during my segment to visualize a point. It meant the viewer could see as well as hear the point I was making.

Props can be great for interviews as well, just don't get carried away.

The first thing to remember is that the prop should be something that can be easily held, like a loaf of bread. Too big and it becomes a distraction or difficult to hold. Too small, and it won't be seen during the interview. It needs to be simple and easy to understand. If the prop requires a long explanation or has too many elements, it just isn't effective.

When using a prop during an on camera interview, you'll need to raise it up. Most people instinctively will hold things just above their belt line. For a prop to be effective in an interview it should be at least chest high.

Only hold on to the prop while you're talking about it. Set it down for the rest of the interview so you don't end up stilting your hand movements.

And don't be offended if the reporter asks if they can borrow the prop for a live shot or standup. You may have done a great job, but the reporter is looking for something they can use to dress up their portion of the story.

It's actually a compliment.

Your idea was so good the reporter had to use it!

THE PROCESS

#21
UNDERSTAND THE MEDIA

Whenever I hear people make a comment (good or bad) about the media, I nearly always hit them with one question: What media? That's because people often throw everyone on TV, or radio, or newspaper, or YouTube, or blogs or one of a dozen other outlets, into the same bucket.

In reality, they're not all the same and they shouldn't be treated that way. If you're about to do an interview it's critical that you understand which media branch you're dealing with.

For example, there's a huge difference between the host of a national TV talk show and a local TV reporter. Yes, they're both on television, and they may talk about current events. But their jobs are completely different. Talk show hosts are entertainment. Their job is to say or do something that is provocative. News reporters generally have a different role. They focus on facts and their final product will be edited. Many use the Society of Professional Journalist's code of ethics.

Sometimes people don't understand the difference between a newspaper's editorial staff, which is supposed to write opinion, and the newsroom staff, which strives for objectivity.

Bloggers, on the other hand, don't need any structure. They often have an agenda or perspective. It might not be something negative, but it will always color their interviews.

The term *media* is incredibly broad with each one focused on a different concept of delivering their content. As a result, before you decide to do any interview, make sure you understand which form of media is asking.

#22
LEGACY MEDIA MATTERS

Let's have a quick review of the various types of media.

Legacy media is the stuff that has been around for a long time. It's television, newspapers, and radio. While some people consider cable TV networks new media, in reality they're closer to legacy media these days.

New media is stuff like podcasts, blogs or online channels. It's amazing how many platforms exist and how successful many of them have become. They range from amateurs to major media companies.

Social media includes outlets like Facebook, Twitter and LinkedIn. News is included in their streams, but social connections are the primary purpose.

With everyone talking about new and social media, some people might question why you might want to spend time talking to a TV station or a newspaper. The answer is in the numbers. When it comes to readers, watchers and listeners, legacy media are still the big dogs. While lots of people no longer have newspaper subscriptions, they regularly turn to their hometown paper's website to get the latest news. The same is true for local TV news. Fewer viewers for their TV channels, and more for their websites.

While many people today say they get their news from social media, the reality is that *the original source* of that story is highly likely to be a legacy media outlet. Obviously, that may change as time goes along. For now, it's important not to discount the impact of doing an interview with a legacy news outlet.

#23

Beware of Off the Record

News reporters, like all professionals, have their own jargon and terminology. Some may ask you to go off the record. It's important to have a clear understanding of what that does — and doesn't — mean, and why it's almost always a bad idea to go along.

Information is either on the record, on background or off the record. On the record is where the material is attributed to you by name. Background is information a reporter can use, but not name you as the source.

When a journalist asks you to go off the record, it's because they're trying to gather sensitive information. They realize that you won't likely want to be quoted. It's not a trick. What they're hoping is that you will point them to material or to others who can offer information. They're hoping you will take them through a door that keeps the story on track, just without your fingerprints.

If you personally know and trust the journalist involved, a request for off the record information might be something to consider. However, if you don't, it's a hazardous request and one that you would be better off declining.

Sometimes, in the course of a conversation, it's not clear what's on the record and what's not.

That lack of clarity can lead to a bad outcome.

That's why you need to assume everything is on the record when talking with a reporter.

#24

BREATHE!

In most conversations, when we get asked a question our first reaction is to blurt out an answer. Normally, that's not a problem. But if you're being interviewed by a reporter, the first thing I want you to do before you answer is to stop… **and take a breath**.

It shouldn't be a long breath, nor should you make a big show out of it. Just take a brief moment to inhale and exhale.

That breath is important for two reasons.

First, you're going to need some air for your answer. Being interviewed for the first time can be a bit nerve-wracking. What you don't want to do is get out of breath halfway through your first response. Taking that breath not only gives you enough oxygen, it's also a relaxing moment before you start.

The second reason may be even more important. While taking that breath only took a brief moment, it gives you a chance to gather your thoughts before you answer. Odds are, the first thing that comes to your mind is the right thing to say. But there are times when a momentary pause allows you to edit the answer. Perhaps it's finding a better choice of words. Or it might be omitting something that is either irrelevant or might cause controversy or pain.

Your brain is capable of processing thoughts at amazing speeds. Take advantage of that momentary breath to let your brain do its work.

#25

BRAIN FREEZE

Brain freeze is that moment after someone has asked you an important question and your mind just goes blank. Maybe you weren't focusing enough on what they were saying. Maybe you're afraid to give an answer that might hurt your situation. Maybe you just went blank because it happens to people all the time.

I remember having serious brain freeze once while doing a live shot during a newscast. I looked into the camera for what seemed like an eternity (it was probably just 5 or 10 seconds) with no idea what I was going to say. It's happened to just about every broadcaster, professional speaker, and actor/actress on the planet.

So, don't panic. There's a simple way out.

Brain freeze is primarily a concern during live interviews. If it's being recorded for later, the reporter or editor will likely cut that part out. That's assuming, of course, that the freeze wasn't a material part of the interview ("Did you embezzle $30 million dollars from your company?"– followed by a long pause.)

If it happens during a live interview the easiest and best thing to do is simply ask the interviewer to repeat the question. That buys you a few seconds to get the gears in your mind to re-engage. If it's not a confrontational situation, most interviewers will actually try to help get you re-started.

Of course, the best way to avoid brain freeze is to stay focused on the interview. If things do clog up, restating the question is an easy out.

#26
EXPECT TO BE INTERRUPTED

You've just launched into a wonderful answer to the reporter's question. Your eloquence is literally flowing forth. And then suddenly the interviewer says, "Yes, but…"

While most people try to avoid interruptions in normal conversation, interviews are not really normal. Whether it's a live interview or one that is being recorded, the reporter usually has limited time. Don't assume they're deliberately being rude. If they think you're wandering down a path that isn't giving them the information they need, they will interrupt. And they might do it over and over again. It could be because you're trying to avoid the answer, but it's more likely that the reporter is focused on a particular angle and wants to keep you focused as well.

I simply point this out to tell you that you shouldn't get frustrated. If you're on live TV, this is the time to look and sound calm. Just move on to the next question. If it's obvious the reporter wants shorter answers, then make them shorter.

If it's not live, you can play it slightly differently. Pushing on and ignoring the question is not particularly productive. The reporter has made it clear that your current answer doesn't interest them. If the comment you were making is particularly important to you then you'll need to figure out how to squeeze it in later in the interview.

So, while you're prepping for that upcoming interview, just remember that interruptions are part of the game.

#27

LIVE VS. RECORDED

Doing a live interview is like performing on a high wire without a safety net. You don't want a hard landing. There is no do-over if you make a mistake or have a mental lapse. The good news is they'll use everything you say. The bad news is they'll use **everything** you say!

That's not meant to discourage live appearances. It's just a reminder of the need to be prepared. After all, television reporters deliver hundreds of live reports a year without harm to their career, health or wellbeing. The live format can be compelling and is greatly valued by television producers and executives.

By contrast, a recorded interview is much more forgiving and carries greater flexibility for both journalists and interviewees. If you're being interviewed and you slip up, for instance, it's perfectly acceptable to ask the reporter and/or photographer if you can answer the question again. Yes, a do-over. Journalists don't want to have to edit out a mistake. They would prefer a clean sound bite to work with because it saves them time and extra effort.

There's also a hybrid which is when something is recorded as live. It may not be airing as you speak, but there won't be a chance to stop and start over. This is especially common for podcasts. They'll be recorded one day and be streamed another (not to mention being available for months or years).

Going live puts a premium on preparation. When you agree to the interview make sure you start by asking, "Live or recorded?"

#28

Look at the Interviewer

Being interviewed is a test of your communication skills, and one way you can strengthen them is to develop the habit of establishing direct eye contact with the journalist who is asking the questions. You're often better able to understand the nuance of the question by observing the interviewer.

I'm not talking about trying to maintain a direct, continuous gaze. People don't naturally communicate that way, and it would be awkward, to say the least, to engage in a staring contest. It's natural for all of us to look away from time to time while composing a thought, reaching for an additional detail, or transitioning to a new point in the discussion. However, keeping consistent eye contact is an effective way to establish a personal connection, control the pacing and keeping the interview process running smoothly.

Watching the other person allows you to better read their tone and intentions. If they're not understanding what you're describing, they'll telegraph that with their expression and body language. That'll give you the chance to change course and come up with an answer that clarifies and is more effective. It allows you to also signal non-verbally that you've concluded your answer.

Watching the interviewer yields other clues that allow you to calibrate your answers. Are they impatient, amused, aggressive or genuinely engaged? Look for those signals that allow you to be more responsive in answering the questions and keeping some degree of control over how the interview unfolds.

#29

WHERE TO LOOK IN THE STUDIO

If you're asked to do a television interview, there is a chance that it will be live. And while it's important that you be prepared with the messages or viewpoints that you want to convey, a key factor in a successful interview has to do with knowing where you should look.

It's not as intuitive as you may think. What you want to avoid is looking in the wrong place or at the wrong camera, since that would make you look distracted and odd (and draw viewer attention away from what you're saying).

Here's a rundown of the different live situations you could face, and how to make sure you stay on target:

Live in studio – There are typically three studio cameras that capture different angles. To avoid confusion, look directly at the anchor who is asking the questions. Don't get distracted by all the studio monitors that show what's being broadcast. While you may be tempted to look directly into the camera, don't. The moment you shift focus to the camera being used, the director might cut away.

Live in the field – If the camera and live truck come to you for a live interview with an in-studio host or anchor, you'll look directly at the camera. Just imagine that there's a person on the other side of the lens.

Live via Zoom – Address the lens at the top of the screen at all times.

Remember, it's not just the message, it is also the delivery that matters in a visual medium like TV.

#30

UNDERSTAND THE DEADLINE

University libraries see it every year; students spending late night hours trying to complete an assignment by the assigned deadline.

Racing the clock serves to focus the mind. It's an enforced discipline, which those in the journalism field know all too well. Impatience is a characteristic of the profession, and for good reason. Don't make your deadline (**miss your slot** is the term used in broadcasting) and you've earned deep ire from your editors and producers. It's an unforgiveable act in the media world.

Those consequences help to explain why journalists' requests typically are urgent in nature. It's why one of the standard questions you or your support staff should ask when fielding a media request is, "When is your deadline?"

If that deadline is unrealistic given your circumstances, it's a good idea to let the media outlet know that. Of course, that can have consequences. Just know that they will write their story with or without your input. And that means you've lost an important opportunity to educate, inform and/or influence a certain audience.

If you're able to accommodate the interview request, it's important to respect the deadline. You may not have all the information at your fingertips, or someone else in your organization may be a better interview subject. If so, simply let the journalist know that. But it's critical that you then honor that obligation and follow up.

Your respect of the deadline reflects your professionalism and will pay dividends, either that day or in future coverage.

#31
You're Always on Camera

Television reporters are always on the hunt for a colorful, memorable sound bite. And it was frequently my experience, as reporter, that it would pop up once the formal on camera interview was over.

What do I mean? It's standard practice at the end of an interview for a reporter to chat a bit with the interviewee. If you've done interviews, you've seen this. That chitchat or banter is done for a couple of reasons; first, just a chance for some small talk or quick fact-gathering, and second, it gives the photographer time to shoot some cutaways—different angles of the interview that help them in the editing process.

Because the formal question-and-answer session is over, it's natural to relax and engage in conversation. The interview, or at least the formal part of it, is over. Always keep in mind that whatever you say during this period, assume that the camera is rolling and the mic is still on. That means it's all fair game.

You can see the obvious risk here since you're being conversational and you may utter some thought that may be more candid than intended. Reporters prize candor and unfiltered comments but letting your guard down can be chancy. By the way, there's nothing unethical on the reporter's part in terms of using what you've said. You just have to understand the rules of engagement.

It's a good reminder that you're always on camera and on the record, even when the interview itself appears to be finished.

#32
SURVIVE A NEWS CONFERENCE

News conferences are a time-honored tool designed to distribute information to a wide audience in a time-efficient manner. Imagine the alternative, saying the same information over and over in individual interviews, as opposed to a group setting. But while they are handy, they can also veer off course and be risky too.

The best way to survive a news conference is to develop a specific plan, which includes messaging and the sequencing of speakers. That organization matters because the last thing you want is the embarrassment, in full view of reporters, of having speakers jockey for position or to step on somebody else's lines.

Communications experts develop what they call a **run of show** which includes the order of speakers, how they transition from each other and the narrative that each is expected to deliver.

Keep the schedule tight and limit the number of speakers. Reporters, who are always facing deadlines, will grow impatient and their questions will reflect that.

You should always anticipate tough or challenging questions beforehand, and know how to answer them or, if you can't, bridge to a key message. Remember that good reporters don't like the idea of being spoon-fed material and can be expected to probe.

More and more news conferences are live streamed these days. Unlike the old days when just the highlights made the news, there's a viewing audience that can watch every moment. So, make every moment count.

News conferences are valuable opportunities, but they require substantial preparation to be successful.

#33
STAY IN THE MOMENT

You've agreed to be interviewed about your company's new water conservation policies. You know the subject matter cold, including the key points you want to emphasize. But as the interview progresses, you may find yourself mentally reviewing the completeness of your previous answer. You might be cringing inwardly because you feel you stumbled a bit. Did you forget to mention the various customer rebates that are involved? Or on the other side of the spectrum, are you trying to anticipate what the reporter's follow up question might be? Or maybe you're just second guessing what you chose to wear.

If you engage in any of those habits, you aren't allowing yourself to stay in the moment. You aren't focused on answering the question that's before you at that point. And that's where mistakes are made.

By not staying in the moment, you're letting yourself get distracted. While that may not be as dangerous as operating heavy machinery in a distracted state of mind, it can still lead to painful results. You may give bad information or maybe just lose your train of thought.

The most proven way of staying on the tracks is to listen, and I mean really listen to the question. Don't spend time thinking about the rest of the interview. This is especially critical if the interview is live. If you find yourself distracted in a recorded or print interview, refocus by having the question repeated.

Pay attention to the questions. Reporters will notice. And the interview will be much more successful.

#34
KNOW YOUR MEDIA PROTOCOL

We can schedule a great many things, but for the most part, media inquiries are not among them. The whole nature of the news media revolves around unpredictability and spontaneity. As the day unfolds, news breaks out, and any sense of organization often goes out the window.

That means when you do receive a media call, whether it's a crisis situation or a question about policy, it's important to know what to do in an efficient and prompt manner.

Without a protocol in place, you're asking for trouble. The last thing you need is to be figuring out on the fly who is authorized to answer questions and what the approval chain looks like. That's how bad information gets into the public sphere.

When a call comes in, you should have an organized procedure with basic steps that include asking which media outlet is reaching out, what the topic is, and the deadline. Your plan should designate the proper spokesperson to channel the inquiry to. That person should have internal contacts to quickly gather information. Even if the answers are not immediately known, it's important for the spokesperson to return the media call to acknowledge the inquiry and let them know that information is being collected.

Always remember that reporters will cover the story with or without you.

Unless you follow up in a timely manner, your organization risks losing credibility and worse, missing the opportunity to communicate in a meaningful manner.

#35
PHONE INTERVIEWS

A lot has changed in the media world in recent years: the rise of digital channels, the constant deadlines, a perpetual news cycle and the increase in competition for consumer attention ... but one thing has not changed. Phone interviews remain one of the simplest and most straightforward ways to interact with journalists.

Yes, it's still okay to talk directly with another human being!

With rare exceptions, phone interviews are used primarily by print and radio journalists. Both love the immediacy involved. But there are some key tips to keep in mind when engaging in this manner.

If you're talking to a print reporter, the primary advantage of talking by phone is your ability to refer to your notes. That provides a certain level of confidence.

This does **NOT** mean that you should be reading from talking points. Journalists can tell when you're simply reciting from a cheat sheet as opposed to answering in a conversational way. The notes are there for reinforcement or a reminder, not as a substitute for preparation or knowledge of the topic.

For radio, be aware that you should be using a landline, not a cell phone. Radio producers and interviewers don't want to worry about noise or a drop in the connection, especially if the interview is live and not recorded for later use. Radio also values brevity. Save the details for the print outlets.

Phone calls are useful and prompt. Alexander Graham Bell would be proud.

#36

Editorial Boards

The media world has changed. Newspaper editorial staffs have shrunk and have less time and space to devote than in the past. Still, spending time in front of an editorial board, which is responsible for publishing the newspaper's opinions, remains an important opportunity for communicating your cause or project.

Keep in mind, if you do, that these interviews are unlike most others. The editorial board will be writing an opinion piece or commentary, which means the questioning will be aggressive and will reflect a point of view. It's not quite a firing squad, but there will be some incoming fire.

In some ways, it's similar to a job interview. Your job is to convince board members that they should "hire" your issue, not somebody else's.

One way that I've helped clients prepare for these sessions is to set up what is euphemistically called a Murder Board. Simply put, this involves developing a list of the most difficult or provocative questions that you may encounter. What are your weaknesses or vulnerabilities? What would your opponents say? How would you counter that?

It can be intimidating to walk into a metropolitan newspaper and face off with its aggressive editorial staff. Practicing ahead of time what points to make, what proof points to offer and your best arguments for refuting criticism will make the discussion productive.

It's often difficult to predict what side the board will take in its commentary. Focus on what you can control: making a good case.

#37
Controlling an Interview's Tempo

Experienced reporters are often expert interviewers, but that doesn't mean you can't take proactive steps to control the tempo or the pace of the discussion when the time comes to sit down for the interview.

Keep in mind that you are the subject expert. That's why the journalist has come to you. In today's media world, reporters who are well-versed on a particular subject or beat are found most often at the networks and large newspaper staffs. But they are shrinking in number, especially at the local level. Instead, it's much more common to find reporters who are "general assignment," meaning they might be covering airport travel one day, city council the next and state budget negotiations the day after.

That should give you, as the subject expert, some confidence to control the interview's tempo and ensure that your key points are imparted.

Some reporters use a rapid-fire technique. They're in a hurry or they may use that as a way to throw you off-balance. You can counter that by slowing the delivery of answers, communicating that you want to arm the reporter with pertinent data and facts, not just reverting to some off-the-cuff sound bite.

You may encounter an interviewer who takes a slow, measured approach. They may hope you'll fill the silence with unfiltered information. Again, you can counter this by asking if there's anything you can do to clarify your answer.

Don't hesitate to offer key points without being asked. Taking steps to control or manage the tempo of the discussion is a successful strategy.

#38
BREAKING NEWS BROKE YOUR STORY

In the news world there's a word that is often used to describe a story of significance that just happened. It's called breaking news. Unfortunately, this term is being overused these days, especially on national cable news outlets.

Real breaking news is when something happens that is so significant it requires immediate attention. Many a day I was sitting in the newsroom working on one story when suddenly I found myself in a car, a plane or a helicopter heading out to the scene of a fire or natural disaster. I have literally been in the middle of interviewing a person for a story when suddenly I had to stop the interview and leave on a moment's notice.

While it's annoying for the reporter to suddenly have their day thrown into chaos, it's especially frustrating for the person who lost their chance for an interview because of breaking news. Your staff worked hard to get that coverage. You studied all morning so you'd have just the right information. You wore the perfect clothes. Then, in an instant, your opportunity was gone. The reporter might reschedule, or they might not. Higher powers will likely make that decision.

I tell you this so that you understand it can happen.

It's not a daily occurrence, but it's not rare.

You didn't do anything wrong, and there's not much you can do to change the situation. Just understand that when news breaks, sometimes your story gets broken.

THE PLATFORM

#39
THE INTERVIEW STARTS AT HELLO

It's important to understand the rules of engagement when meeting with a member of the media. When it comes to a newspaper reporter, be aware that the interview doesn't start when the tape recorder is turned on or when the questions begin — it starts the moment you say hello. Every bit of it is on the record.

Reporters are trained to observe and note details about their surroundings. The story they write doesn't depend on just the question-and-answer exchange itself. They're looking at what's on the wall or on your desk in your office, how you may be interacting with others in your office and any other factors that may flavor what they write.

A newspaper reporter who once visited my desk in the newsroom to prepare a profile story about how I approached my political coverage noticed a photograph tacked up by my computer. It included a humorous "caption" that had been made up by the press secretary who had given me the picture as a sort of gag.

That caption, although fictional, sparked some questions about whether it truly represented part of my thinking about a competing reporter. It didn't. I assured him it was just a joke, and that's how it was treated in his story.

This is not to say that print interviews are based on a gotcha approach. Still, it's always best to be aware that there is often much more to these interviews than just a standard list of questions.

#40
How Much Detail to Offer?

Not all media platforms are created equal. Since television, radio, newspapers, blogs and podcasts have different needs, your approach to an interview should reflect that. You need to understand how much detail each will want before you begin.

Newspapers remain the most likely place where you'll need to be prepared to go into detail. Newspaper reporters are often assigned to a beat or specialty—such as education or politics. Be prepared for them to ask more specific questions and follow-ups. They have the time to do this and the space to write more complex stories. They're trained to think with more detail and will appreciate what background you can give them.

Blogs are similar to newspapers except that their audience is often narrower. You'll likely have the opportunity to give more details in a specific area.

Broadcast reporters don't have the luxury of detail, even if they think that way. Television journalists have punishing deadlines, often multiple times per day, and must write much shorter stories. TV reporters depend heavily on visual elements. Radio reporters are always on the hunt for good sound that improves their story.

Podcasts are generally long form. Depending on the hosts, you'll be able to give plenty of details. Just remember, it needs to be interesting. The details need to tell a story.

Print reporters may also ask for more numbers. They may hand those off to someone else in the newsroom who create charts or infographics.

These different mediums reach different audiences. Tailor your answers accordingly.

#41
PAINT A PICTURE

Radio interviews are often quick and relatively simple. Whether they're effective depends on how descriptive you can be. Because we're only dealing with audio here, there are built-in limits to capturing your audience's attention. It's best to appeal to what's called the **theater of the mind**.

To do that, keep in mind the importance of not just telling a story or delivering a key message, but doing it in a way that paints a visual for the listener. That can mean using figures of speech to spark the imagination.

Former CBS News anchor Dan Rather was known for his colorful metaphors that served to illustrate a point. Some examples:

- Shakier than cafeteria Jell-O.
- This situation in Ohio would give an aspirin a headache.
- This race is as tight as the rusted lug nuts on a '55 Ford.

This type of language may be too folksy to work for you, and it's always important to speak in a way that is authentic to *your* style. The point is to think of how to describe something in a different and captivating way.

- It was like trying to bail out the leaky boat with a thimble.
- Think of 50,000 Big Gulps, and that gives you a sense for how low the lake level is.

There *is* a line between corny and creative. However, using visual phrasing and expressions can be enormously effective in making sure that a radio interview is memorable and impactful.

#42
Email Interviews

In recent years, interviews conducted via email have become a standard practice. It reflects the increased number of deadlines journalists have to meet to fill newscasts, newspapers and digital platforms.

It wasn't so long ago, however, that reporters wouldn't agree to this form of interview. From their perspective, it's much more limiting compared to a phone call or in-person session since it prevents a traditional back-and-forth dialogue and follow-up questions to seek clarification. Experienced journalists want those follow ups. Reporters viewed an email exchange as non-responsive and too controlled.

That began to change and become more accepted in Washington D.C. as agency spokespersons and political press secretaries at the federal level started to use the format more often as a matter of convenience. Journalists dropped some of their previous objections in acceptance of practical deadline concerns, and now it's relatively common in newsrooms at all levels.

The advantage of an email interview is obvious; you're able to craft answers to specific questions and you have a record of what was said if there's a dispute later about accuracy. You have some advance time to think about what you want to disclose or communicate.

Just be aware that there are some drawbacks. You're not able to develop a relationship with the reporter because of the impersonal nature of email. Those relationships are important for future stories. And you also miss the opportunity to steer the journalist to another story, or a better one because of the one-way nature of the exchange.

#43
USE A LANDLINE

Using cell phones are second nature. They've become an appendage to our body—the way most of us communicate with emails, text and phone calls. They're how we stay connected. It may surprise you, then, to hear that there's a specific type of media interview where grabbing the cell phone isn't a good option.

Radio stations have traditionally expected to conduct interviews by landline, and they ask you in most cases to honor that request. It was considered a best practice and had everything to do with quality. More recently, stations have also begun to use digital channels to record their interviews. Whether by landline or online, remember that radio is an audio medium, and that it's important to their audience to listen to a broadcast that is clear and uninterrupted.

The last thing radio listeners want is to hear is an interview that is spotty and inconsistent. That is a good way to invite the audience to tune out.

I'm no engineer, but cellular service depends on radio waves, which has the inherent risk of signal breakup or drop off. The metal and fiber used in landlines mean they're a much more reliable platform, and thus a preferred choice for interviews.

Is using a landline essential? **No**. You may not have access to one, especially if the interview request is urgent. Online portals are a growing option. Keep in mind that online or landline will result in a cleaner interview.

#44

Smiling for Radio and Podcasts

Radio and podcast interviews are great mediums for expressing yourself and telling your story. You still have to know how to be effective in communicating on the radio which starts with how listeners respond.

The radio audience, like most podcast listeners, can't see you. They miss the gestures and facial expressions that you might use to make a point or add emphasis to an answer. That lack of a visual cue is a disadvantage. But there's a technique you can use to counter that, and to ensure that what you say on the radio is compelling and impactful.

When I first worked in radio news, I learned an important lesson from Larry, the afternoon disc jockey. When I spoke directly with him, there was nothing notable about the conversation. Yet on the air, he was dynamic. He captured your attention. **How?** What I realized while watching him was how he made effective use of facial expressions to enhance his delivery.

When Larry opened the microphone, he would smile. His face would light up. That enthusiasm translated directly into what he said. If he was happy, or funny or earnest, his expression conveyed that tone. It was like a magic trick.

No one is suggesting that you become a professional radio announcer. But adopting a facial expression to calibrate what comes out of your mouth is a great way to ensure that the listening audience will remember what you had to say in the interview.

Having that impact, after all, is the point.

#45

KNOW THE SHOW

There's always an initial surge of excitement when you're asked to do an interview. After all, this is a chance to get your message or story in front of a larger audience. But before you say yes, make sure you understand what kind of program or article will use your interview.

The easiest requests to answer are when the interview will be used in a broadcast or print news story. If that's the case, then you just want to know the focus. That doesn't mean you should say no if you believe it could be negative. After all, this could be your chance to change someone's perception of your company or industry. You just want to understand the risk potential up front. It's helpful to know a little bit about the reporter who will be doing the interview. Are they known for hard hitting questions or did they just graduate from journalism school last month?

If it's a TV talk show, make sure you know what type. Is it a Sunday morning news review or a public affairs show? Are you the only guest or will there be others?

Things get even more complicated if it's a podcast or a blog. Before you say yes, do some research. Is the host or writer the friendly type or confrontational? Do they always take a specific spin? How big is their audience?

Knowing the show isn't a guarantee against unwelcome surprises, but it will definitely reduce the risk.

#46
Zoom Interviews

It's more and more common to see TV interviews done through Zoom or some other video conferencing service. In many ways it makes life easier for everyone. The reporter doesn't have to spend time driving all over town, and interviews can be done from anywhere. That's great, but it means you're now solely responsible for how you look and sound.

First, your background is especially important. Your normal office might be fine for video conferencing people in your workplace; you want it to be exactly right if you're going to be on TV. Simpler is better. You don't want something behind you that distracts from your message. That includes people, pets and strange artwork.

Next, make sure your camera is at eye level. We shouldn't see your ceiling, your floor or your double chin. Also, make sure you're looking directly into the camera and not the picture on the computer screen. People trust you if it appears you have eye contact.

Your face needs light. Even a simple desk lamp will help. Just try not to make it too harsh or just from one side. Put a little makeup powder on your face to reduce the shine.

Finally, you want to sound good. While some computers have great microphones, others sound lousy. If you plug in an external microphone, it will probably sound better.

Zoom calls also give you the option to use the audio from your phone. Sometimes that actually sounds better.

#47
Podcast Interviews

Podcasts are everywhere these days. The most recent estimate put the number of active podcasts worldwide at 850,000 with more than 30 million episodes available. More than half of Americans over the age of 12 say they listen to podcasts.

I use those numbers to make it clear that when someone calls you about being a guest on a podcast, it's something you should seriously consider.

Of course, not all those podcasts are the same. While some have millions of listeners, most have very small audiences. Still, it's a chance for you to get your message in front of additional people so why not say yes?

Just make sure you understand both the program and the host. Is it just a fun conversation, or is the host controversial? Is the audience narrowly defined by demographic, interest or profession?

As with all media interviews, remember your goal. Are you promoting your career or is it a chance to talk about your organization?

Podcasts are longer so you'll get the chance to tell stories. Just remember to keep them short. Better to have the podcast host begging for more than wishing you'd stop droning on with too many details.

Have notes handy with both facts and your key messages. The longer the podcast, the more important it is to be able to come back to those.

And finally, if you're hoping to do more podcast interviews, invest in a good microphone. It's one less barrier between your message and the audience.

#48
SHORT MORNING SHOW INTERVIEW

Interviews on TV morning shows are wonderful opportunities. You'll usually get three minutes of live television. Three. Your comments won't be edited. Everything you say will be beamed to thousands of homes.

That's the good news. The bad news is that you only get three minutes, and all of your comments (both smart and stupid) will be heard by people in those thousands of homes.

While a three-minute interview doesn't seem like a big deal, it actually requires the most preparation. The three minutes will include both your comments as well as the news anchor's intro and questions. That means you're lucky if you have two minutes. And trust me, it goes quickly.

You need to know your message completely. You need to make sure that you slide it in as quickly as possible. Yes, you need to answer the questions, just remember to include what is important to your organization. You won't get a chance to say something again, so you need to do it right the first time.

Don't be offended if the news anchor knows extraordinarily little about you or your organization. There were plenty of times I anchored a morning show and didn't get the prep material in time to read before show started. I met the interviewee for the first time during the commercial break, had a minute or two of chit-chat and then went live.

Three-minute TV interviews require focus and prep. Make sure you have both.

#49

A 30 Minute Talk Show

These days 30-minute talk shows could be TV, radio or podcasts. Whatever the medium, the ground rules are the same.

The first thing you want to ask is whether there will be other guests. If it's a two-sided issue and they represent the other side, then it's not really a talk show, it's a debate. It might still be a great opportunity, but debates require lots of preparation. You don't want to sound like you don't know the issues. Don't treat the opportunity casually.

If the other guests are just there to add additional insight, then it's no longer a debate, it's a competition. Your job is to create the perception that you are clearly the expert. You have the most relevant and insightful comments.

You don't get that status by droning on after a question. Even though 30 minutes seems like it will allow you to get in every detail, once they put in the commercials, anchor intros and questions (which can sometimes last forever) and comments from other guests, that time can fly by. Assuming it's not a hugely complex issue, your answers should last 30 to 45 seconds. If the moderator wants more, they'll follow up with another question.

Unless it's a critical point (or a debate) try to avoid cutting off the comments of the other guests. It's no different than a conversation at a party. No one likes a blabbermouth who dominates the conversation.

#50

A 60 Minute Interview

These days the place you're most likely to get a 60-minute interview is for a podcast. While the rules are similar to a 30-minute interview, there are a few important differences.

Research shows that average length of time spent listening to podcasts is 22 minutes. That means you need to make sure that you get your most important messages in the first third of the program. That doesn't mean you need to cram all of them into the first 3 minutes. You just want to make sure that you've hit the high points early in the program. You can go back later to add more detail if necessary, but the important messages have to come in the first 22 minutes.

It's not unusual for a podcast to have a single guest. That means you'll be doing a lot of talking. While a good host will have plenty of great questions to fill up the entire podcast, there might be times when they ask you to elaborate. That doesn't mean it's your chance to dive into the detailed deep end. Keep the jargon to a minimum and make it easy to understand. Use the time to tell effective stories.

One other thing to remember during long interviews is that you don't want to get too loose. The last thing you want to do is something that you might regret later on. Stay focused and remember that every comment will be part of the program so use them wisely.

#51
ARE TRADE INTERVIEWS DIFFERENT?

News media organizations are not cut from the same cloth. Trade media outlets are a completely different creature from other mainstream media organizations, and thus the way they conduct interviews is different as well.

For starters, trade media is designed to be read by insiders. They are not a general interest publication. Their reporters start with a strong base of knowledge about a particular industry or profession—such as business or utilities. That actually makes your job easier. If you work for a water company, for example, you typically won't need to provide the same kind of background to a trade publication that you would for a general assignment reporter from a daily newspaper. The trade publication reporter will typically have written before about rate cases and how regulatory agencies affect your company's affairs. They already will likely have a good foundation for understanding and writing about your particular issue.

Another significant difference is that trade media will often be willing to provide a list of questions in advance for an interview, whether it's conducted in person or on the phone. Some are even willing to send a list of questions that can be answered entirely through email. Some trade associations will also ask you to provide photographs for their story instead of using a staff or freelance photographer.

Don't assume that you're going to get friendly or soft treatment from trade media. However, it's useful to remember that in preparing for an interview they already speak your language.

THE MESSAGE

#52
YOUR GOAL

Before you agree to any media interview, it's important to understand your goal.

In some cases, the goal is obvious. You're promoting your company's new product, or you've just written a book. This is your chance to tell people about it through what we call *earned media*. That's TV time or newspaper column inches that tell your story without you having to pay any money. Ask any author who has been in Oprah Winfrey's spotlight how much it affected sales and you can instantly understand why it matters.

Other times, it's a little more complicated. For example, you might be in a situation where doing the interview will help your company but hurt your reputation. Or you might be in a situation where the person from the media outlet interviewing you has already made it clear that they have serious questions about something you've done.

I'll make it clear right now that I'm usually a fan of doing the interview. Done properly, it's your chance to get your part of the story out to the public. Turn it down, and you've missed the opportunity. I've seen some impressive examples of people who have actually turned public opinion because they did a difficult interview.

Just make sure that first you understand what you're trying to achieve. What is the key message you want to get across? Are you promoting the company or yourself? What are the potential downsides? The more you can concentrate on your goal, the easier it will be to do the interview.

#53

Focus on Your Message

Your interview with the news media may be something you've wanted, or something you're dreading. Either way, it's important to focus on what you're going to say. Before you start talking with a reporter, you want to plan out your message. After all, that's why you are doing the interview in the first place.

The first thing you need to understand is that your message needs to be boiled down to its most basic elements. You won't get 20 minutes to explain how great your company might be or why a particular problem happened. You'll need to think in terms of sound bites or quotes. Short, concise statements that contain your key points.

Of course, that assumes you know what you want them to be. That's why it's critical you think about what message you want to get across during the interview. Brainstorm with your staff, or at the very least, write down a list of bullet points. Once the ideas get flowing, boil them down to your three key points.

When the interview begins, you may be answering a wide range of questions.

As we mention elsewhere in this book, it's important to answer the questions you're asked. But at the same time, you need to focus on how each answer relates to your message. That doesn't mean you need to work the same three sentences into every answer, but you want to make sure that you're focusing on the message that matters to you.

#54

How to Pivot

During the course of any interview, there are moments of opportunity and moments of risk. You should always be looking for the chance to insert your primary message. Another challenge is that you may get asked questions that you simply are not in a position to answer. It may be sensitive information or material that's not ready to be released publicly, or you may simply not know. That's okay. Good reporters are supposed to ask questions that probe and challenge.

The best way to handle these situations is not to shut down, but to learn how to pivot. Also called bridging, it's one of the most useful tools you'll use in media interviews.

Just like a real bridge, bridging can get you from an unsafe to a safe place.

Let's say, for example, that a superintendent is asked how many schoolchildren are going to be harmed by a new budget that cuts funding. Instead of accepting the premise that kids will be hurt, the superintendent says children's education is always the district's top priority then pivots to a discussion of how they've also avoided layoffs or school shutdowns which would really impact kids. He's changed the course of the conversation from an accusation of harming children in his district to ways in which they've preserved student/teacher ratios and smaller class sizes.

Use phrases such as, "what's important to remember" or "what I can tell you" to help you pivot and stay on solid ground.

#55
Why 'No Comment' is a Loser

Want to make sure your interview gets included in tonight's news?

Just say, "No comment."

You've agreed to an interview because you want to set the record straight, you want to offer your organization's perspective and you want to provide some facts that tell your story. The last impression you want to leave is evasiveness or a lack of transparency. That would negate the whole purpose of the interview.

That's why serving up the response *no comment* is generally a bad idea. Secrecy, or the appearance of it, is not a good look. Many people have a belief that the person saying this awful phrase must be guilty of something.

The good news is that there are lots of ways to essentially provide no comment without actually saying so. Yes, everyone understands there are things you can't talk about. Matters under litigation and issues dealing with personnel decisions are always sensitive and can't be discussed. The best way to handle those questions is to explain that the lawyers won't let you talk about it, then pivot to one of your key message points.

Sample: "I can't violate attorney/client privilege, but the important thing to know is that we are determined to serve all of our customers' needs now and in the future."

That way, you've found an opportunity to express that point, while also avoiding the trap of appearing to be evasive. It's a much better tactic than sounding like a rerun of *Law and Order.*

#56

OFFER SOLUTIONS

News stories are often constructed like mini dramas. They can include a victim, a hero and a villain. Many stories are built around conflict or a problem. Journalists are often interested in looking for a solution to that problem as the narrative unfolds, and if you can offer that, it makes your interview especially effective.

There was a case I covered where a notorious serial killer was arrested years after the crimes were committed. It turned out that the breakthrough in solving the case had to do with pursuing genetic clues on genealogical websites; clues that identified family members and eventually narrowed the search for the suspect.

After the suspect pleaded guilty to the crimes, I interviewed the chief prosecutor who understood the importance of outlining a solution that went beyond this individual case. The new DNA tracking technique not only solved the case in question, the prosecutor said, but was a revolutionary new tool that was already being used to solve cold cases in other parts of the country.

This law enforcement official went beyond the typical discussion about evidence that closed a specific case and framed their investigative technique as holding widespread value for catching suspects who had evaded detection for years. That larger solution made the story much stronger and more impactful.

Not every topic has a straightforward solution but look for ways to offer one as a way to move the story forward and enhance the importance of your interview.

#57

COLOR, NOT PLAY-BY-PLAY

The most effective interviews create a memorable impact with the use of clear, descriptive language. To become good at that, I've found that it's useful to borrow a concept from sports coverage.

Simply put, depending on subject matter, you want to play the role of the color announcer, not the play-by-play guy or gal. Here's what I mean...

When I was a reporter and would respond to a fire, I would be looking for quick information from a public information officer. Frequently, they would convey the basic who-what-when facts of the incident: We've all seen these interviews on the news:

> We responded at 1100 hours with two units Code 3 to the 1200 block of Gateway. We found one structure fully involved. Nobody was home, and we contained the fire within 20 minutes.

It's all useful information in the above play-by-play format. Sometimes you'd have the good fortune of finding an official who gave you color commentary:

> Given all the dry brush around the property, it could've taken down part of the block. Heavy smoke made it as dark as night, and made it hard to tell, at first, what we were dealing with. But our crews made quick work of it, and everybody is safe.

Now that was descriptive, not just dry facts, and made telling the story more impactful. Not every story lends itself to this color. Interviews can be more interesting if you can paint a picture rather than spew facts.

#58
How to Apologize

It's always been amazing to me how many politicians and elected officials fail to understand a fundamental dynamic: people are willing to forgive. An earnest apology can rebuild trust. Cover-up or refuse to accept responsibility, and the downward slide begins.

There was a case once where a state legislator found himself arrested by an undercover officer in a prostitution sting. For several days he sequestered himself in his apartment making no appearances. His office issued only a cryptic statement about a mistake being made.

Eventually, he got some wise advice. The next day, he called a news conference that included prominent members of his political party from the region as well as family members. There, the accused lawmaker issued not a denial, but a full-throated apology.

He apologized for his behavior and his lack of judgment. He apologized in particular to women voters in his district and offered no excuses.

Instead of seeing his career crumble, this politician was re-elected and eventually moved on to higher office. His earnest apology didn't exactly mean a clean slate, but his words led voters to forgive him.

Hopefully, your need to apologize won't come as the result of a prostitution sting. No matter the mistake, the process is the same. Accept responsibility for what you've done and make a sincere apology to those affected.

Yes, the media will pound you and the internet will never let it die. But a sincere apology has the power to defuse the immediate media storm. Just make sure it's done quickly and with no ambiguity.

#59
YOU ARE THE EXPERT

You just got a call from a reporter who wants to come by to interview you today. While some people may go into panic mode, I want you to take a moment to feel good about yourself.

As a reporter, I worked long and hard to find just the right interview for a story. Sometimes I'd talk to a whole series of people before finding the perfect person. I wanted to speak with that individual because they were the expert.

You aren't likely to be asked to talk about subjects you don't understand. You've been singled out because of your knowledge on a particular topic. Many times reporters are working on a story they know little about. This is your opportunity to educate them on a topic that matters to you.

Of course, you don't want to get cocky.

A reporter doesn't want to get belittled for their lack of knowledge nor do they want a lecture with incredibly boring detail. All you have to do is listen to the questions and give answers that will help the TV audience or newspaper readers understand what may be a complex subject.

Most important, you should relax with the knowledge that you were chosen because you're the expert.

Sure, there are plenty of little things we talk about in this book that will make things easier. Bottom line is it's your background and experience that will help you navigate the interview.

#60
USE ANALOGIES

As Forrest Gump would say, "Life is like a box of chocolates. You never know what you're going to get."

Forrest was a pretty simple guy so that analogy helped him understand the complexity of life. Turns out we all need a way to make something understandable and analogies are usually just the right tool.

If your subject matter is complex, an analogy will go a long way in helping the reporter understand and, in turn, the people reading or watching the story. The simpler the analogy, the greater its impact.

Building an analogy is simple. The easiest method is to connect two concepts with the words …is like… followed by a statement that explains. Here's an example, "A good analogy **is like** a window cleaner, it just makes everything clearer."

Analogies work best when they compare or contrast. They're also most effective when they're something that is easy to understand. The movie *Dumbo* has a song that says I've "…seen 'bout everything, when I seen an elephant fly." It paints a picture that everyone can understood.

Don't expect a great analogy to just happen during an interview.

Great analogies, like great speeches, take time and effort to create. Before your interview think of a way to take the most important point you want to make and create a simple analogy. Try it out on a few people to make sure it works.

The analogy will not only help make your point; it will also make you quotable.

#61

BEWARE OF SPECULATION

My job as a reporter was to find answers. When there were no answers, I often asked people if they'd be willing to take a stab at what an answer might be. In the absence of facts, all it takes to create a story is a qualified person who can speculate about what might happen.

Speculation is dangerous territory in a news interview. It puts you into the position of basically reading your crystal ball to come up with an answer. Sometimes that's easy to do. After all, two and two will add up to four. But there are times when your speculation could put you on shaky ground.

If you're going to speculate, you need to do it strategically. How will your speculation affect your organization or your reputation? Do you have enough information to come up with an educated guess? Do you work in a regulated industry where making a speculative answer could have negative impacts?

There are times when speculating will promote your brand. Often times the reporter will make it clear that your vision is important because you're the expert. Of course, there are other times when speculation will cause problems. How many times have you seen politicians mocked because they speculated on some issue they really knew very little about?

Just remember, your answer will be quoted and remembered. You don't have to be an expert on everything. Just make sure that speculating advances your brand and doesn't hurt your image.

#62
NUMBERS ARE GREAT

One of the reasons I went into journalism is that I can't do math. But that doesn't mean I don't like numbers. In fact, I love numbers and so do most reporters.

If you're prepping for a news interview, make sure you have a few great numbers to quote. In a perfect world, those numbers are fresh and new. They're something that hasn't been published before or at least aren't generally known. Truthfully, however, just about any number is great. It gives the reporter a fact that they can use in the story. It's something that will make you look and sound like an expert. Most importantly, the numbers will help the viewers and readers understand the story.

The double-edged sword with numbers is that they have to be accurate. A good reporter will check to see if your numbers are right. That's great if they are, and a problem if they're not. Suddenly you go from being the expert to a person who doesn't know their stuff. Your numbers may be used against you to show that you were trying to slant the story away from the truth or that you hadn't done your homework.

Most important, if you don't know a number, don't speculate.

Tell the reporter you'll be happy to research the correct answer and call them back. Once you give a number, reporters will take it and use it as foundation for their story.

Make sure those numbers build your reputation instead of knocking it down.

#63
TAKE A POSITION

If your goal is to say something memorable in an interview with the news media, then you're going to need to take a position. You're going to say why you support or oppose something and back it up with facts.

That's not to say every interview requires you to take a position. It's possible that you're simply being interviewed as an expert who can explain options or scenarios. Just understand that the reporter asking the questions will likely want your opinion about the issue at hand. You need to plan ahead so that you're ready for the question and know how to respond.

You'll want to choose your positions strategically. Give too many, and you have no idea which will be used. Say it poorly, and it won't supply the needed sound bite or quote.

Your position needs to have some value. If you just say you support sunshine and apple pie, the reporter will likely be thinking, *So what?* News time and print space is valuable. You'll want to make sure your position is worthy of the reporter's investment.

Your position statement will likely only last 10-15 seconds. It has to make clear where you stand and also *why* you believe that way.

You may have opportunity for follow up, but you need your position to be clear and thoughtful. Make sure it's something you understand and believe because once it's published you may spend a lot of time defending your comments.

#64
IS IT A CRISIS?

There are really two kinds of media interviews: Crisis situations and everything else. Some people might think that any time the media shows up at your door, it's a crisis. Really, that's not the case. A true crisis is when something has happened that is going to affect people or the environment and involve health or money. Plus, it's a situation in which your comments to the media will have direct impact on others.

Let's take a quick moment to give some historical context. The original Greek meaning of the word crisis actually refers to a turning point. By definition, it is not something bad. The way you deal with the media during a crisis could determine the severity of the impact the crisis will have on your organization.

In a perfect world, your organization has a crisis communication plan. You've identified a spokesperson and have a set of guidelines already established. As soon as the crisis hit you've been referring to your crisis communication plan to help you plan on what to say to the media.

If you don't have a plan in place, you're going to want a strategy before you start doing any interviews. You don't have a lot of time, you need to make sure that you've both gathered information and formulated a message.

You probably won't be able to wait until all the facts are gathered. The news media are likely doing their story with or without you. Getting your message ready quickly allows you to impact the story and public perception.

#65

CLOSE WITH A KEY MESSAGE

You've got a key takeaway message in the interview that you're about to give. Of all the points you plan to make, there is one that is central and that you're hopeful will be used by the news outlet. It's not productive to try to tell the reporter what to write. That attempt to control the story never plays well and is guaranteed to create resentment. However, there are ways to amplify the importance of that key quote you're offering.

Don't be bashful about returning to that point during the interview if the opportunity presents itself; the more times you say it, the greater the odds that it takes on greater prominence and will be used in the story. Don't be heavy-handed about it because that can backfire, but look for an appropriate moment to refresh the message.

If that moment doesn't surface, don't despair. You'll be ahead of the game by keeping this in mind: it is extremely common for reporters to conclude their interviews by asking whether there's anything you'd like to add or whether there's anything else that needs to be addressed.

This is sort of a catch-all habit that journalists develop and use as an insurance policy to give them confidence that they haven't missed something.

It's an open door that you should sprint through; the ideal opportunity to come back to your key point.

Be prepared to capitalize on that moment and cap the interview with your coveted takeaway.

THE INTERVIEW

#66

AN INTERVIEW IS NOT A CONVERSATION

Interviews, whether they're for broadcast or print, can take many different forms. They can be freewheeling in nature, wandering down different tangents without specific boundaries(as in a personality profile). Those are the exceptions.

For most news stories, interviews are structured and designed to glean information in a relatively controlled setting that respects any time constraints of both parties. Those are the interviews that you're most likely to experience.

One thing those interviews are not is a conversation. They are an exchange of information. The exchange itself may be conversational in nature, *but don't be fooled*. It's a transactional arrangement, with both sides expecting value.

The way these interviews are carried out will vary considerably, depending on personality, comfort level, whether those involved know one another, and the nature of the topic itself. Is it a light feature about weed-eating goats, a standard story about the release of new health data or a crisis subject related to a product recall?

As the person being interviewed, it's useful for you to remember that this is not a conversation. It's a reminder that will allow you to keep your guard up and not volunteer information that you shouldn't.

Ideally, you'll both achieve your goals out of this transaction.

You'll provide the facts or messaging that you felt were important. The journalist will harvest information to tell a solid and substantive story. And you won't end up in hot water by forgetting this wasn't just a neighborly chat.

#67
ANSWER IN COMPLETE SENTENCES

Just about every time I did an interview during my TV news career I always gave one instruction before the camera started rolling.

Answer in a complete sentence.

Most people don't realize that when we're having a pleasant conversation, we often give answers that are just fragments of sentences.

- "When are you going on vacation?" "Thursday."
- "What are you having for dinner?" "Spaghetti."

It works fine because everyone in the conversation hears both the question and answer. They understand the context.

But a TV or radio interview will be broken down into sound bites. The reporter's question will often be clipped off. That partial answer makes it tougher for the reporter to write the story. They really want to use that great comment, but because it's incomplete it just doesn't work the way the story is written.

Fortunately, this is an amazingly easy problem to fix. All you have to do is use the question in your answer. If they ask, "When did the accident happen?" your answer should be, "The accident happened to me last Thursday."

Why does it matter?

Remember, your goal is to get your message across. Giving your answer in a complete sentence makes it ever easier for the reporter to properly quote you. Reporters are looking for great quotes or memorable sound bites. Giving them answers in a complete sentence helps ensure that your comments will be used accurately.

#68
ANSWER THE QUESTION

It's hard to trust someone who won't answer a question. It taints the way you view all of their other answers. That's why it's critical that you give an actual answer when you're asked a question in a media interview.

For years, there was one school of media training which basically said, "Don't worry about the question, just give them the answer you've prepared."

That's a huge mistake.

I'm not saying you have to spill your guts and give every detail for any question. You do need to make sure you give a reasonable answer. Not answering the question makes you look evasive and people start wondering what you're hiding.

There are times when a rookie reporter might just let your non-answer slide and move on to the next question. However, if it's an experienced reporter you'll not only get asked the same question again, but they may start calling you out for dodging the question. Your non-answer suddenly sounds silly and you're getting publicly called out for refusing to answer.

Besides, there are many ways to answer a question without telling things that you shouldn't.

If a reporter asks how much money the CEO embezzled, it's perfectly acceptable to say you are still investigating to determine what, if anything, was taken. You may still get asked the same question several times, but people at home will give you the benefit of the doubt if they believe you're sincerely answering the question.

#69

BE HONEST

You've just been asked the one question you didn't want to hear in a TV interview. It could be about how your CEO is being investigated for sexual harassment. Or maybe it's about a chemical leak that's going to cause major environmental problems.

Your gut reaction is to avoid the truth. That could be a huge mistake.

Secrets are hard to keep these days. We live in a Wiki Leaks world where incriminating emails bounce through a lot of inboxes. As much as you want to think that you can hide certain facts away, it's getting harder and harder. You need to assume that the truth will eventually come out. And when it does, anything you did to cover that up will damage both your organization's reputation as well as your own.

There are lots of examples ranging from the Catholic Church's pedophile priest problem to Volkswagen's diesel emissions disaster. Leaders thought they could avoid problems by hiding the truth. It not only didn't work; the organizations were badly damaged.

That doesn't mean you have to say everything you know during the interview. Just don't lie. There are plenty of ways to answer a question without divulging every detail. Yes, the investigation is ongoing. No, you don't know where it will lead.

Whether it's an interview for network TV or a small-town newspaper, it will be posted for all the world to see.

You don't want to tempt someone who knows the truth to show you lied.

#70
AN INTERVIEW ISN'T A DEPOSITION

While an interview with the news media may seem like a legal deposition, it's important to understand that they're vastly different. You could say that the ground rules for both are the same. You'll want to tell the truth and stay calm. You'll want to prep so that you're ready for the questions. And yes, what you say can be used against you.

Often times a deposition is an adversarial proceeding. The attorney wants to get information from you that will aid their case and potentially hurt yours. I've read some deposition advice that makes it clear your job is absolutely not to help the person asking the questions and that simple yes or no answers are best.

While some news interviews may seem adversarial, most are purely informational. The reporter is doing a story and you have insight into their topic. While the attorney in the deposition may have done massive amounts of research before the questioning begins, often times a reporter didn't know they were doing a story until just a few hours before. Anything you can add that will help them understand is usually greatly appreciated. During my reporting career I did plenty of interviews that changed the focus of the story because of a helpful interviewee.

Because this interview may boost your reputation or help your company, simple yes or no answers are never enough and could make you sound rude.

#71

KEEP IT SHORT AND SWEET

No one likes a person who just won't stop talking. It's annoying at a party, and it's also a problem when you're doing a news interview.

You're the expert. That's the reason the news media is interviewing you. That doesn't mean you need to tell them every single detail about what you've accomplished or what needs to be done. Most news stories don't have the time or space to dive too deeply into the nit and the grit of your world. The reporter's job is to take what they learn from you and turn it into something that every viewer, listener and reader will understand.

Try to make sure your answers don't go longer than one minute. Shorter is better. If the reporter needs more information, they can ask a follow-up question. If it's a live interview, keep your answers *even shorter* and don't go longer than 30 seconds. Don't be too short or abrupt. Make sure you answer the question fully and in a complete sentence or two, just keep it nice and concise.

Keeping your answer short helps you in several ways.

First, it forces you to focus your comments and keep your priorities in order. You'll do a better job of giving an answer that sums up what really matters.

Second, it will also help keep you out of trouble. The more you ramble, the more you might say something that you didn't mean to include or give an off-hand comment that could cause a problem.

#72
ANSWER EVEN WHEN YOU CAN'T

Just because you can't give an answer doesn't mean you can't answer a question. There's a definite art to answering a question without actually including sensitive or controversial information.

Sometimes it's because you just don't have all the facts. Other times it might be information that you can't divulge. You certainly don't want to lie, so be prepared with things you *can* say which can address the questions without giving specifics.

You've no doubt heard plenty of interviews after some crisis or tragedy that sound like this:

> Our thoughts and prayers go out to those affected by this tragic event. This flies in the face of all our company values. We're absolutely looking into what happened and whether we could have done anything differently. In the meantime, we're doing everything we can to support those who were affected.

It says something without saying much.

That doesn't mean the reporters won't fire back questions looking for more specifics. I've been in plenty of news conferences where the person answering simply makes it clear that information isn't available and then goes on to explain some other aspect of the situation.

What you don't want to do is just say that you can't answer that question. That might work for some law enforcement situations, but if you're the spokesperson for an organization you'll likely want to sound like you're being as helpful and open as possible. Just understand that doesn't always mean telling everything you know.

#73

Loaded Questions

In talking to journalists, you should always be prepared for the times that they will pitch you some loaded questions.

You may know the type — questions that already assume a conclusion or judgment has been made. Like a major leaguer at the plate facing a knuckleball or a wicked curve, you just have to know how to read it as it is coming at you.

Here's an example. A surgeon who is testifying at the Capitol on behalf of a medical trade association against a bill that would require an extra specialist be on hand for a certain procedure. The bill is supported by family members who say reform is needed to prevent deaths. The association's argument is that the extra assistance is not necessary and would make the procedure unaffordable for too many families. A reporter pulls the physician aside and asks, "What chance does the family have when they're up against a group of wealthy, politically-connected surgeons?"

It's a loaded question, designed to provoke a defensive response.

The reporter is hoping for a retort or sharp response that will make the surgeon appear thin-skinned. The best response the physician can make in this case is to ignore the bait, then to calmly note that he is not a political player, but a medical professional who's speaking from firsthand experience about the bill's impact. He's not buying into the suggestion that the political system is unfair, he's talking about flaws he sees in the legislation.

Learn to watch for loaded questions and you'll avoid the trap they represent.

#74
CRISIS INTERVIEWS

When the media calls during a crisis, you don't have to give them answers immediately. Just understand that the longer you take to respond, the less likely it is that your comments will become a part of the initial story (or their immediate social media posts).

If you're ready to do an interview, then dive right in. If not, take the reporter's name and number and tell them that you'll call them back shortly. Give them a specific timeframe and then live up to your promise. If you don't call back in the correct time, they will assume you've blown them off and will start writing their story without you. Even if you're not ready to do the interview when the promised time arrives, call the reporter and tell them it will take slightly longer. Just understand that in some situations the reporter may have an editor or producer breathing down their neck demanding something that can be posted or aired.

Once the interview starts, everything you say is on the record so be cautious. Stick to what you know and don't speculate. If you don't know the answer to a question, tell the reporter you'll find the information and send it along.

After a huge oil spill in the gulf, British Petroleum CEO Tony Hayward famously said that after dealing with the crisis he wanted his life back. He was mercilessly skewered.

Remember, your interview is a turning point. Use it to improve the situation and not make it worse.

#75

CAN I START OVER?

There's just something about talking to a journalist that causes some people to trip over their own tongue. They may know the topic completely, but once the interview begins, it all comes out in a jumble. They desperately want a do over.

If that happens to you, I have great news. In most cases, it's perfectly fine to ask if you can start over. Of course, there is one major exception and that's a live interview. The moment you started talking everything was being heard by thousands of people. The best you can hope for is to get yourself back on the rails and try to sound like you have it together. While a podcast isn't always live, the expectation is that there won't be any editing so you must treat those interviews as if they are live.

If the interview isn't live, then everything is different. I used to love when the person I was interviewing would ask if they could say something slightly different. Maybe they realized they were too wordy or just didn't make a clear point. If they thought they could do it better, I absolutely was going to give them the chance. That didn't mean I would ignore some incriminating statement. It just meant that I was happy to let them make their point in a way our audience would understand. It makes for better sound bites and better quotes.

Should you find your tongue tied up in knots and feel frustrated that you can do it better, just ask. Reporters will nearly always say yes.

#76
Don't Repeat a Negative

Your organization is facing a very controversial situation. The news media shows up to interview you and they immediately start with a hard-hitting question such as, "Isn't it true you lied to protect the company image?" Because your first thought is to correct the reporter, you respond, "No, it isn't true we lied to protect our image." You then go on to give a series of facts about what actually happened.

But when the story appears on the news that night the first sound bite is simply the portion where you say that you didn't lie to protect the company image, which implies you lied for another reason!

It's critical when you're facing this type of interview that you don't repeat a negative. Doing so creates a series of problems. It reinforces what the reporter just said. Now you're the one talking about the company's lies. You inevitably sound guilty of something because you're on the defensive. The only question becomes: why did you lie?

Earlier in this book, we talk about the importance of incorporating the reporter's question into your answer. **This is the one situation where you absolutely don't want to do that.**

Yes, you want to get the correct information into the interview. Just don't do it by repeating the negative or incorrect comment.

Skip directly to information about how your organization took immediate action to correct a problem or how you're looking into what happened.

Don't repeat something that could only make you look bad with a very small edit on the media's part.

#77
No Jargon!

Every business has its own language. Sometimes it's filled with long complex terms, other times it's acronyms that make no sense in the real world.

When it comes to jargon in your news interview—I have one word of advice: **Don't!**

Even if the reporter knows enough about your industry to slightly understand your lingo, there's a good chance the audience won't. That's true even if the interview is for a trade publication. You want to make your points in a way that anyone can understand what you've just said.

This isn't always easy. After all, jargon is the language you use every day. You've probably reached the point in your career that you don't even notice when you're slipping into complicated terminology. You'll have to actively think about how you can take your complex lingo and convert that into words that anyone can understand.

I'm not saying you should dumb down your interview. The best communicators are the ones who can take complex subjects and make them understandable. You can still cover intricate concepts, just do it with normal words.

Before your interview begins, practice by explaining something to your spouse or even your children. Do it over and over until you're comfortable without the jargon. When you arrive at the interview make it clear to the reporter that if you should slip into jargon that you actually want them to ask for a simpler version.

After all, your interview is worthless if it can't be understood.

#78
ANSWER THE TOUGH QUESTION

Media trainers will talk a lot about bridging and pivoting. How you can almost seamlessly slide from a topic you don't want to discuss to a different issue. While that's a great tool that can help you sidestep a thorny subject, there are times when you're just going to have to answer a sensitive question.

It might be because the reporter has done their homework. They know exactly the right question to ask and they're not going to get distracted by a smooth answer. They'll calmly keep coming after you until you're backed into a corner. It could happen at a news conference where every reporter has a different version of the same question.

A common rule in the world of crisis communication is that one of the first things you must do is accept responsibility. If your organization is at fault, you have to fess up. If something bad happened, you don't want to sound like you're hiding from reality.

It's tough when you're standing there facing a reporter and having to bare your soul. But sometimes, it just has to happen. There will be times when you can't get on to explaining the next step until you answer the question.

Hopefully, this is something you've planned for.

You've thought about what you're going to say and how to say it. That doesn't mean you have to give every detail, but you'll have to say enough in your answer to satisfy the reporter that you're not dodging the tough question.

#79

Candidate Interviews Are Different

I covered a candidate for statewide office once who expressed her distress about how difficult her media interviews had been and how critical the coverage was soon after the election was over.

This candidate had been a high-profile leader in the business world and had grown accustomed to positive news coverage about her company's growth, its earnings, hiring record, and other developments. There had been some negative stories, but they were more the exception than the rule.

Why had her experience with campaign coverage been so different?

The fact is, political journalists are a tough crowd, in keeping with the profession they cover. They have a responsibility to vet all candidates. They are going to take a much more challenging and cynical look at a candidate's background and campaign promises. After all, there's a lot at stake.

If someone is running for election, political reporters are going to be looking for flaws in each carefully crafted biography. If the candidate has a spotty voting record, or hasn't released tax records, or has a history of lawsuits, it's going to get written about.

Also the candidate's opposition will be actively looking for flaws and weaknesses that they can exploit and send along to journalists covering the campaign.

For all those reasons, candidate interviews are different from other news coverage. Business reporters or other beat reporters produce a different type of story than political reporters.

Running for office is not supposed to be easy. Just ask a political reporter.

#80
It's Okay Not to Know

You work for a prominent trade association and have been contacted by a journalist who is looking for information on how, let's say, the local business outlook is going to be affected by a potential move of an area sports team to a different city. Negotiations with the team's owners are underway and you're prepared to talk about the impact on retail and hotel trade.

When it comes time for the interview, the reporter asks those questions as expected. But they're also looking for some inside perspective on the closed-door talks between the team's owners and the league.

You might feel a natural inclination to want to be helpful. In fact, you're flattered to be asked. But that doesn't mean you should feel obligated to engage in on-the-record speculation about what may be happening. That is basically known as gossip, and quite often it does you no good to engage with topics you have no solid or direct knowledge of. If it's wrong, your credibility takes a hit and it'll cause blowback for your organization. If you are right, there are still some in your community who will think you are too free with your information.

You might be able to refer the reporter to someone who is better qualified to answer a question, and that always makes for good media relations. **Always remember that it's okay not to know.**

If you can get the information, but don't have it at hand, say so. Then always follow through.

There's enough risk in this world already without guessing or speculating.

#81
NAIL THE DISMOUNT

Have you ever noticed that gymnasts talk a lot about nailing the dismount? Even though it's just one element in their routine, they work long and hard to make it exactly right. That's because the dismount is the last thing the judges will see before giving a score.

Psychologists have a concept they call the Peak-End Rule. Basically, it means our minds can't remember everything, so we generally only recall the peak moments of a conversation or story ... and the end.

When you're doing an interview with any news media, you first want to create peaks. Moments when you say something significant or at least smart. Hopefully, they'll be so good that the reporter will feel compelled to use them.

While you can't always predict what others will view as the peaks, you do have some control over the end.

Both print and broadcast reporters will often ask if there's anything else you feel is important to add.

If you're on live TV it's quite common for the interviewer to say something like, "And finally..." That's your cue to say something memorable. Yes, you have to answer their question, but you can do it in a way that reinforces your message.

Don't be afraid to say something like, "Here's the takeaway..." You may have said it earlier but give it one last boost. And since it's the last thing the viewers will hear, both psychologists and gymnasts will tell you that it has greater impact.

THE REPORTER

#82
REPORTERS: ENEMY OR FRIEND?

Neither.

Reporters are trained to find, write and tell the news of the day. They have an important role to play, have a strong sense of right-and-wrong and believe in their First Amendment mission. The best ones are skilled at uncovering information that wasn't apparent or was actively hidden then developing a story they believe will be of interest to their readers, listeners and viewers.

All of that is a way of explaining that **reporters are not your enemy, but they are also not your friend.** In my years of working in newsrooms, I found that the vast majority were focused on meeting their deadline, staying out of trouble with their editor or producer, and telling a story that is fair, compelling and accurate.

Some are friendly and accommodating, some are aloof and demanding, some are all business. No matter the style or personality, ultimately their allegiance is to the public. That is their client and that is who they answer to, not you or your particular set of concerns and issues.

It's important to keep this dynamic in mind in order to avoid misunderstandings. A reporter may be sympathetic to your cause, but don't expect them to write the story the way you want. They aren't just note takers. That's called stenography. Their job is to follow the story wherever it may lead.

Understanding their mindset explains why it's always wise to use appropriate caution with media inquiries, and to calibrate your expectations about the result.

#83

UNDERSTAND THE REPORTER

Working as a reporter these days isn't easy. The website 24/7 Wall St put together a list of the 25 worst jobs in America. Newspaper reporters were number 3 and broadcasters were number 8. Career Cast lists reporters as having one of the 10 most stressful jobs in the United States. That would be okay if the money was great, but it's not. Investopedia says the average annual salary of $43,640 is wedged in between social workers and ministers.

And it gets worse. Moneywise ranked 27 professions for respect. At the bottom of the list, right behind members of congress, lobbyists and car salesmen, were reporters.

Every day is stressful for a reporter. Yesterday's story is old news and they need something new today. They have 8 hours in which to research a topic, find someone to interview, perhaps drive to multiple locations and then write and edit the story to meet their deadline.

Why do they do it?

As a former reporter, I'm pretty biased here. I believe that journalism is a truly honorable profession. Known as the fourth estate, it is the check and balance on all things public. It strives for accountability.

While few people are perfect, the reporters I've worked with are ethical and believe in finding truth. Yes, their employers need to improve ratings and circulation, but the journalists' job is to tell factual stories.

When the reporter calls, just take a moment to think about their complicated daily life, and then answer their questions.

#84
Journalists' Code of Ethics

I'm sure there are more than a few people who are going to sneer when I say this, but true journalists have a code of ethics. I say "true" journalists because there are lots of people pretending to be journalists these days, and they're not. The digital world has given various folks a platform. They might host talk shows or podcasts. They might have a blog or a YouTube channel. They specialize in commentary, not journalism.

I will, however, quickly admit that the journalistic code of ethics is not a mandate. It's aspirational. Reporters don't have to get a license so they won't lose it if they slip up. The code is also open to interpretation and vagueness which is always complicating when it comes to ethics.

I point this out just to make it clear that there *are* standards. When a reporter misses the mark, you have every right to speak to their editor or news director and ask for an explanation.

Here is the code:

Members of the Society of Professional Journalists believe that public enlightenment is the forerunner of justice and the foundation of democracy. Ethical journalism strives to ensure the free exchange of information that is accurate, fair, and thorough. An ethical journalist acts with integrity.

The Society declares these four principles as the foundation of ethical journalism and encourages their use in its practice by all people in all media.

- Seek truth and report It
- Minimize harm
- Act independently
- Be accountable and transparent

#85

DEADLINES NOT AGENDAS

Occasionally during media training, clients will express worry about whether they'll be treated fairly by the news media.

Having worked in television newsrooms for several decades, I can tell you that the vast majority of reporters are hard-working, well-trained professionals who believe in serving the public interest. They've been educated about the responsibilities of journalism and the need to follow ethical standards. They are interested in providing balanced information and keeping viewers informed. Much of their day is spent trying to meet their deadlines and staying out of trouble with their editors and producers.

Story selection and placement are subjective, it can cause suspicion. It's not unusual to hear people ask if reporters are pursuing some political or social agenda. I always answer that in order to have an agenda or to pursue some specific conspiracy, you would have to be organized, and if you've ever seen a newsroom in operation, organization would not be what comes to mind.

No two days are the same. Things often get left out of stories due to a lack of time, not an agenda. Much of the time, newsrooms are about barely-controlled chaos, with reporter assignments changing throughout the day and assignment desks juggling crew logistics to meet the deadline demands.

Journalists are attracted to the profession because they believe in challenging the status quo, in shining light in dark corners, in asking challenging questions.

Very rarely is there a political or nefarious agenda. Just a need to meet deadlines and, maybe, get a lunch break.

#86

Beware the Blogger

The blogosphere is an amazing world. It's a diverse spectrum of people writing about all kinds of stuff. But just because someone is writing about something based in fact doesn't mean they're a journalist. In fact, many bloggers have a specific agenda and goal that they weave around facts.

If someone calls you saying they're working on a blog article, my advice is to get their information and the name of the blog and then call them back. Take a few minutes to then look up the blog and see what topics are covered, their target audience and how the individual blogs are written.

Some bloggers use strong journalistic principles. They try to accurately portray all sides of an issue in an unbiased way. However, there are plenty of bloggers who write specifically so they can further their own opinions and agendas. Some bloggers have huge audiences and others are rarely read by anyone.

Once you understand the blogger and their style, that's when you can decide whether it's worth your time to participate. If it's obvious that the blogger's perspective is different than yours and that they've written articles in the past that aren't positive, you should take a pass. On the other hand, if it's a fairly written blog or at least one that supports your issue, go for it.

Don't think because a blog has a small following that it won't matter.

Once your comments are in the blogosphere, they live forever and might come back to haunt you some day.

#87
KNOW THE INTERVIEWER

When I first started working in the TV news business, one of our reporters was a grizzled journalism veteran named Gene McLain. Although Gene was about to retire, he was still a true news hound. Gene loved nothing more than to dig through the outer layers of a story to find the hidden truths. And while he was rather small, Gene had a gravelly and somewhat gruff voice that could truly terrify potential interviews. In truth, he was a gentle soul, but Gene wasn't afraid to ask tough questions. If he showed up at your door, you'd better be prepared to answer.

On the other hand, if I was the reporter assigned to your story back then, you were going to get a hugely different experience. Sure, I knew how to ask who, what, when, where, why and how. But I didn't have the experience to pound away when something wasn't quite right.

If knowing your message is the most important thing you can work on before your interview, knowing something about the reporter should be second on your list. Is it the person with the tough questions or the new kid on the block?

Before they show up, spend a couple of minutes researching their stories. Get a feel for the way they write or how they ask questions.

Finding out early that the interviewer has a tougher tone is a lot better than discovering at the last minute you're going to get grilled.

#88
REPORTERS REPEATING QUESTIONS

As a reporter, I always had a list of questions in my head, still, there were situations where I would pose the same question over, perhaps several times, during the course of an interview.

No, it wasn't just forgetfulness, although I've been accused of that. Sometimes it was to probe for consistency. Other times it was in hopes that the second answer would be more concise or more passionate. And sometimes it was to probe to see if the interviewee really knew the subject matter.

There was a particular deputy press secretary who worked for the governor of my state, and occasionally he would get assigned to carry out a requested interview. The problem with this spokesperson was that he wasn't confident enough to really answer questions. He had a couple of talking points or canned responses he had memorized. No matter how many times I rephrased my question, he would give the same stock answer, word for word. He had no credibility to me, and his interviews had little real value.

There was a state legislator who in one interview gave an evasive answer to a question about offshore oil drilling. He got the same question over and over. He was consistently evasive, and all those answers showed up on the air that night.

The point is that reporters may repeat questions if they perceive a wall and/or a weakness hiding something. Sometimes they do it just because they are looking for a simpler, clearer answer.

#89

Hostile Questions

It's a common perception; reporters ask negative or hostile questions, so how can I expect to get a fair shake? Why do they ask such hostile questions?

The thing to remember about journalists is that it's not personal. Unlike public relations, their job is not to buy the company line. They are professionals who have been trained to be skeptical and ask challenging and provocative questions. If they simply accept what they are told without some level of critical analysis, they would be stenographers, not reporters.

This point was drilled into me early. When I was still in college, I was sent on a journalism assignment to interview the city's mayor. The topic had to do with a special appointment made to fill a vacancy on the city council. Both the mayor and the new appointee were members of the university's faculty.

When I sat down with the mayor, in addition to asking about qualifications, I also inquired about whether his personal relationship affected his decision to appoint the new council member. Were they mere acquaintances, or were they friends? It was a legitimate line of inquiry because it addressed objectivity. He resented the question and said so on tape. He became angry and his voice shook.

When I returned to campus with the interview, the professor was delighted I had been willing to challenge the mayor. "Your job is to hold politicians accountable," he told me.

It's not personal.

Always assume and anticipate tough questions and keep your temper in check.

#90
AMBUSH INTERVIEWS

Ambush interviews are like spotted leopards. They're rarely seen (at least by most people) yet can be very dangerous.

Ambush interviews happen for one of several reasons. Sometimes, the reporter may have requested an interview but you refused. If the reporter is chasing a major story, they won't settle for no interview. Other times, the reporter knows that once you're aware of their particular story, you'll start circling the wagons and building a defensive wall. They want your first reaction, not the polished one.

Ambush interviews can be a very nerve-wracking experience. Suddenly there's a camera in your face and you're being asked what are likely uncomfortable questions.

You need to take immediate control of the situation. You don't do that by either lashing out or trying to ignore the reporter. First and foremost, don't say "no comment" and keep walking. Earlier in this book we talk about how those words just make you sound guilty.

The absolute best thing you can do is stop and engage the reporter. Listen to their questions and tell them that you don't have all of the information right now, but that you'll be happy to sit down later that day (or very soon) and do an interview. Running away makes you look like you have something to hide.

Stopping and arranging an interview time makes you look and sound very reasonable.

The reporter may keep asking the same question. Your job is to stay calm and make them look unreasonable for not waiting a very short time for a full interview.

#91
MACHINE GUN QUESTIONS

Rapid fire questions are not something that most people will ever have to face. It's reserved for high confrontation situations where the media believes that the person being interviewed has either done something wrong or may be withholding information.

It might be a series of questions without a pause, or they could be leaving you just a brief moment before moving on to the next question so you appear to be dodging the issue. It could happen during a one-on-one interview or it might be during a news conference and you'll feel like a group of people are ganging up on you.

Machine gun questions are more about theater and less about journalism. It's about hurling accusations and watching your reaction. There might even be a hope that, like some witness on a TV courtroom show, you'll crack under pressure and confess to everything.

The first thing you have to do when this happens is the toughest: **Don't get flustered.** Take a deep breath and try to relax or at least look calm.

When the questions stop, you begin your answer by saying, "Let's start with…" and choose the question you want to address.

If you try to answer and the reporter cuts you off with another question, stop talking. Make it clear (without yelling) that you'll be happy to answer when they give you a chance to speak.

Your goal is to look like the rational, reasonable person when the interview finally airs.

#92
DON'T FILL THE SILENCE

We've all been in situations where we've encountered someone who makes conversation easy. The discussion and exchange of viewpoints just seems to flow. Conversely, we know how uncomfortable or awkward it can be to have a conversation with lots of stops and starts. You'll find yourself working to fill the gaps. And while that is natural in most social interaction, **beware:** that dynamic can be risky when it comes to interviews with reporters. **Here's why...**

Many reporters are skilled interviewers; they use a variety of tactics to build stories that their readers or viewers will find interesting. Reporters are always looking for information, and those tactics can revolve around setting the pace of the questioning. That takes us back to how dialogue can flow, or not.

In the course of an interview, a reporter may pause after you've finished an answer. Maybe they're just jotting down their notes, or they're processing what you've said while they're composing a follow-up question. Many times, they may be counting on your impulse to keep talking. That can be a risky move and can result in volunteering information or saying something that wasn't intended.

Remember that you are under no obligation to fill those moments of silence. A better response is to ask the reporter if there's something they didn't understand, or if there's something you can clarify.

That helps you to control the flow of information you're able to share during an interview. That should always be your goal.

#93
The Photographer is Your Friend

If you've ever done a television interview or watched one being done in person, you might not have paid a great deal of attention to the photographer. They are behind-the-scenes people, and many prefer to be that way. The stars of the show, after all, are the interviewee and interviewer.

Don't underestimate the importance of news photographers. They are professional journalists who take care of what's needed for good esthetics. They have the responsibility to deal with lighting and audio quality as well as the framing of the shot.

These photographers have seen it all. They've worked in all kinds of situations, some of them sticky and difficult. Sometimes they work in tandem with a reporter. More often these days, they are sent out solo to capture interviews for use in a newscast.

Always remember, it's a good idea to be kind to the photographer.

Go out of your way to thank them for their efforts. Not only is it the right thing to do, it has other benefits. This person is responsible for how you will both sound and look. They might also edit the story.

All too often, photographers are viewed as just a person behind the camera. Taking a moment to recognize their talent and effort will absolutely affect the final product.

After all, you wouldn't risk insulting a chef before they made your dinner, right?

THE AFTERMATH

#94
DIGITAL CORRECTIONS

Reporters make mistakes. It happens every day. Sometimes it's just a misspelled name, other times it's an incorrect fact.

Years ago, correcting those mistakes was pretty useless. Sure, the newspaper would print a "correction" on the second page, but most people who read the original story never saw the fix. Broadcasters rarely came back to correct a problem unless it required a major retraction.

In this digital world, things have changed. Yes, someone may read the story with the mistake today and never see that a correction was made. Yet now since stories live online forever, you'll want to make sure that any mistakes are corrected for the next reader. And the sooner the better.

In my post-news world, I've worked with many reporters on stories. Often times, the story appeared online before it was in print or broadcast form. That gave me a chance for an instant review. On more than a few occasions I spotted a mistake and called the reporter.

Each time they were thankful that I caught the error and they made the online correction immediately. Often it meant the story that appeared in the newspaper the next morning had the fix.

If something significant changes, the reporter might even be willing to update the content with a new quote or additional data.

Of course, getting a major retraction is a lot more complicated. But if all you need to do is correct basic errors, don't be afraid to reach out right away.

#95

NO GOING BACK!

Your interview was going great. You looked and sounded spectacular. You effectively slid your message in right away.

And then you said *it*. You knew it was a mistake the moment it came out of your mouth. Maybe it was insider information that could hurt your organization. Or it could have been a comment that just sounded insensitive or rude.

The moment the camera was turned off you made what seemed like a very reasonable request. You asked if the reporter could not use that one little comment. After all, it wasn't part of the real message. To your shock and amazement, the reporter looked at you calmly and said, "Sorry. It's on the record."

When you say something, anything, to a reporter, it's fair game. The reporter didn't force you to say it. You did the interview voluntarily. You don't get the right to approve the content of the final story (because no reporter gives that). Don't expect to take it back. **Just making the request creates a problem.** Perhaps the reporter didn't notice the comment or realize its significance. Once you bring it to their attention, they might realize it's something they should use.

I will tell you there were times when someone made that request and I told them okay. But it was generally because the comment wasn't relevant to my story that day.

The best advice is to be careful about what you say before you say it.

#96
WHEN WILL IT AIR?

Television news operates on an ever-changing schedule, subject to uncontrollable events. Reports often have little say about when or if their story makes it on the broadcast. What was scheduled to air at 5pm may get bumped to the late newscast or get dropped completely.

The story or interview you're involved in may get dropped from coverage plans altogether before a reporter even shows up.

I remember a planned news conference at a children's hospital involving a ballot measure with funding that affected healthcare for sick kids. The story received strong interest that morning from the local television stations. Everybody told organizers they were planning to send a crew.

And then, an hour before the event, news broke about a domestic violence scandal involving a member of the city's police department. The police chief was hosting a hastily scheduled news conference at the same time to discuss the trouble facing one of his officers.

Scandal wins over healthcare funding every time. It derailed the planned coverage; all the reporters and photographers were diverted by their assignment desks to the new story.

Anyone who's had many dealings with the media know this is not an unusual occurrence. Reporters get shifted around to new or breaking stories all the time. The point is to be realistic about whether your story or announcement gets covered, and if it is, *when* it may air.

Be aware that news is a messy business and temper your expectations accordingly, it won't always match with your preferred timeline.

#97
Follow Up

You can't be an expert on everything. It's inevitable in talking to a reporter that you'll be asked a question which you can't answer; either because it's something you haven't been cleared to talk about or because — ***gasp*** — you simply don't know.

In either case, you can offer to check on the requested information and either get back to the reporter, or if appropriate, connect them with another individual who has expertise in that area. Just remember that it's important to actually follow up on those items. Don't think that particular part of the story will simply go away if you just move on.

In addition, it's always important to live up to your promise. Fail that, and you'll potentially lose credibility. This is also one last chance for you to affect the direction and tone of the story. Plus, the final version might reflect your failure to communicate. Reporters will see it as a dodge and will call you on it.

I recall a spokesman for a state agency who was blatant about promising to check on details for a story, was well aware of the deadline, and yet simply failed to follow through. That resulted in a story that criticized the department for being unresponsive instead of a routine story about community health data.

The spokesman had done this before. He wasn't doing his job, and his department's image suffered as a result.

It's a simple formula. If you can't answer, say so. If you promise to follow-up, do so.

#98

Watch the Interview

After every concert, rock star legend Prince would get together with his band and watch a replay. They were probably exhausted, but he wanted to make sure they knew what worked, and what didn't.

Any time you're interviewed, it's important that you either watch or read the interview. You want to understand both your performance and how the story was written or edited. You may have thought you were eloquent, yet the reality of the final produce could be something completely different. There are times when you discover the words you used didn't convey the message in your mind. Or that your body language was a huge distraction. Or maybe it's just that your hair was way out of place.

Watch the interview and think about what you can do better the next time. In some cases, it's just refining the message, other times it's understanding that you need to pay more attention to your appearance.

It's also important to watch so you can see how the reporter used your interview. Did they run multiple sound bites from you or just a quick five second pop? While your first reaction may be that the reporter blew you off, it could have been that the way you answered the questions was too wordy or confusing.

Watching the story helps you understand what the viewing audience saw or heard, and it also is great training for your next interview.

#99

THEY ONLY USED 15 SECONDS!

There's a great scene in the movie *You've Got Mail* when Tom Hanks is watching a TV news story about how his family superstore book business is pushing small shops out of business. Hanks' character had done an interview with the reporter so he assumed his side of the story would get equal weight. When he finally appears on camera it's only to say, "I sell cheap books. I do. So, sue me."

His friend and co-worker looks at him and says, "That's what you said?" To which Hanks replies, "That's not all I said." And then adds "I was eloquent!"

There are two important lessons to be learned from that scene. The first is be careful of saying short, overly glib statements. It's highly likely that will be used in the story.

The second lesson is less about what you do and more about how you have to accept. The reporter may interview multiple people in one day for a story and get plenty of quotes or sound bites. Your 10 minute interview may boil down to a 15 second clip. Ideally, you've done a great job refining your message so that the reporter has plenty of great quotes. Sometimes even great comments get cut.

Don't feel shortchanged. It's a function of time and space limits.

Even knowing this, you still need to do the interview.

This is your chance to have an influence on people. One great comment can have a big impact on the audience.

BONUS TIP
ROBOT JOURNALISM IS COMING

You're now reading lots of stories that a human reporter never touched.

A number of artificial intelligence companies have already popped up creating software to write news stories. It might be an item about a company's latest financial earnings, or it could be a story about a sports event. Hiring a flesh and blood reporter to cover little league games can be pretty expensive, so AI generated stories create the coverage at just a fraction of the cost.

It's more than just analyzing data and stats. Some AI services are sending computer generated questions and then inserting the quotes into the story.

So how do you know that set of questions you just received in an email came from a human and not a robot journalist? As I write this, the odds are that the interview request you got most likely originated with a living being. But as we move forward, that will change. The more important stories will get reporters, the less important pieces will be AI.

The good news about AI stories is that there is less interpretation. It will take your quote and insert it into a logical location. The bad news is that you'll get less opportunity to shape the story while talking with the reporter. Some news outlets are using AI for fact checking which is another reason to stay honest.

The robot journalism world is evolving quickly.

Eventually, someone will figure out how to game that system. But for now, treat all interviews the same and read the final story carefully.

Media Interview Work Sheet

WWYHB: What would your headline be? Sum up your story in less than 6 words.

_____

Message: What are the three key points you'll want people to remember?

1. _____

2. _____

3. _____

Sound Bites: Come up with a 10-15 second statement that effectively sums up your message or makes a bold statement about a problem or issue the audience can understand.

#1_____

_____

#2_____

_____

#3_____

_____

About the Authors

Rick DeBruhl is a true media insider.

After graduating with a degree in journalism from Cal Poly San Luis Obispo, Rick worked in radio for a brief time before landing his first television job at KCOY-TV in Santa Maria, California. After less than a year he was offered the opportunity to work at KPNX-TV in Phoenix (back then it was KTAR-TV).

During Rick's 31-year career at KPNX-TV he worked as both a news anchor and reporter covering stories throughout Arizona and around the world. Rick flew fighter jets and crawled through subterranean caverns. He interviewed presidents, rock stars and plenty of everyday people. Rick has done literally thousands of interviews and walked many people through their first media experience. His many awards include three Emmy statues and the coveted New Times Best of Phoenix *Best Anchor Hair* award.

In addition to his local news career, Rick has spent more than three decades covering auto racing and automotive events for TV networks like ABC, ESPN, NBC, Fox Sports and others. He covered Formula One, NASCAR and the Indy 500. He's currently the voice of the Barrett Jackson collector car auctions on the A&E networks so his media work continues.

After Rick left local news, he spent nearly a decade as the Chief Communication Officer for the State Bar of Arizona. He managed a team responsible for media relations, marketing and overall communication. He used his news experience to help him work with reporters in all kinds of situations. As a result, he understands media from both sides of the microphone.

In addition to his undergraduate degree, Rick earned a Master's in Media Management from the University of Missouri. He's certified to handle crisis communications by the Public Relations Society of America.

Currently, Rick is a communication consultant based in Phoenix, Arizona. He works with organizations and individuals to improve their messaging. This includes media training, presentation coaching and crisis communications.

To reach Rick, just go to his website at www.RickDeBruhl.com.

Kevin Riggs brings an insider's perspective to the workings of the media world, with more than three decades of broadcast experience in California as a television reporter. An Emmy award-winning journalist, he spent many years as an anchor and political reporter for KCRA-TV in Sacramento where he covered the state capitol, national political conventions, presidential campaigns and the occasional scandal.

Kevin earned a journalism degree from Cal Poly, San Luis Obispo, then worked for radio stations on the Central Coast for a couple of years, ending up in Santa Barbara.

Kevin then made the move to KCOY-TV. His early political reporting involved coverage of President Ronald Reagan's Western White House visits to his Santa Barbara County ranch, where he was exposed to the dynamics of national politics. He then worked at KFSN-TV in Fresno. Later, after the move to KCRA-TV, he covered the historic election of Arnold Schwarzenegger as California governor in the 2003 recall, traveling overseas with him to Israel for a trade trip the following year.

Other high-profile assignments include the 1995 bombing of the Oklahoma City federal building, the 1999 Columbine school shootings, and the 2000 Florida presidential ballot standoff. Many of his national assignments were for NBC News providing reports for affiliates across the country.

Kevin was inducted into the Mustang Media Hall of Fame at Cal Poly in 2018. He serves on the journalism department's alumni advisory board. He's also a proud winner of the Edward R. Murrow Award for Breaking News, an Associated Press documentary award, and political reporting awards from California State University, Sacramento's Center for California Studies.

Kevin's years of reporting, and extensive interviews, give him a strong understanding of what works in communicating and delivering your message, even as the media evolves with the growth of digital channels.

Kevin puts that knowledge to work daily as a senior executive with Randle Communications where he specializes in helping clients with a wide range of media issues.

He also continues to provide regular on-air and web political analysis for KCRA-TV, his longtime broadcast home.

To connect with Kevin just go to
www.RandleCommunications.com

Made in the USA
Columbia, SC
28 April 2024